WALK TOWARD
THE RISING SUN

WALK TOWARD THE RISING SUN

FROM CHILD SOLDIER TO AMBASSADOR OF PEACE

A MEMOIR BY
GER DUANY

WITH GAREN THOMAS

MAKE ME A WORLD
New York

MAKE ME A WORLD is an imprint dedicated to exploring the vast possibilities of contemporary childhood. We strive to imagine a universe in which no young person is invisible, in which no kid's story is erased, in which no glass ceiling presses down on the dreams of a child. Then we publish books for that world, where kids ask hard questions and we struggle with them together, where dreams stretch from eons ago into the future and we do our best to provide road maps to where these young folks want to be. We make books where the children of today can see themselves and each other. When presented with fences, with borders, with limits, with all the kinds of chains that hobble imaginations and hearts, we proudly say—no.

Text copyright © 2020 by Ger Duany
Jacket photograph copyright © 2020 by Simon Maina/Getty Images
Interior art copyright © by 2020 by Yvan Alagbé
Map art copyright © 2020 by Michael Reagan

Visit us on the Web! GetUnderlined.com

Educators and librarians, for a variety of teaching tools, visit us at
RHTeachersLibrarians.com

Library of Congress Cataloging-in-Publication Data is available upon request.
ISBN 978-1-5247-1940-1 (trade) — ISBN 978-1-5247-1941-8 (lib. bdg.) —
ISBN 978-1-5247-1942-5 (ebook)

The text of this book is set in 11-point Sabon.
Interior design by Trish Parcell

Printed in the United States of America
September 2020
10 9 8 7 6 5 4 3 2 1

First Edition

To my mother, Nyathak,
who never got a chance to go to formal school
to learn how to read and write.

For my sister Nyandit,
who never got a chance to see sunrise, life.
May your spirit live through, and on with,
this memoir.

Dear Reader,

Violence is a strange monster. It takes many forms. From climate change and armed conflicts to pandemics and the small desperations that happen inside people's homes and families. Yet when politicians and pundits talk about trauma or destruction, they most often use the word "war" as a metaphor—wars on poverty, or illiteracy, or disease. But for those who have had to endure actual wars, the small ones or the big ones, the metaphor falls short.

In 2016, I was working with young Syrian refugees in Munich, teenagers who had to flee as the walls of their cities, of their communities, and of their childhoods crumbled around them. They looked at photos from two or three years before and told me that the buildings they posed in front of were no longer there, reduced to piles of bricks and faded photographs. My own understandings of the conflict in Syria, which had to do with everything from global politics to climate change, were useless in the face of these young men and women, who showed me piles of bricks, saying, "This was my home."

If you pull back the lens, to global economies and climate changes, wars look very different, but up close they are the same. Perhaps the most important thing that unifies all these experiences, however, is not the horrors, but the tools we use to survive them. *Walk Toward the Rising Sun,* by Ger Duany, is a remembrance of the tools one young man used to piece together a world that was breaking around him. The friendships, the skills, and the belief in oneself that he had to develop in order to escape circumstances beyond his control became the building blocks of a remarkable life that has taken him around the world as an actor and activist.

There are wars everywhere. Some stretch across nations, and miles of wilderness and culture and families like Ger's. Some smaller and no less important wars rage inside the hearts and heads of young people. There is a temptation to not tell these stories, to provide for young hearts imaginary worlds without conflict. There is also a temptation to assure young people that wars like this happen only in far-off places, to brand anything that is uncomfortable or challenging as "foreign" or "other." War is scary. One of the bravest things Ger talks about is his own fear.

But there is another path—to pull the lens even closer and see how the conflicts that Ger has endured prepared him for the life he would lead, giving back to the many communities he has called home. To see this story, and stories like it, as providing pathways away from the conflict. To draw maps, for ourselves and our young people, that will lead to a place where no war is too far away for us to care about the people involved—maps that will furnish us all with a safe passage to a world in which all these wars are distant memories.

Christopher Myers

MAKE ME A WORLD

This book is a memoir; it is a true story based on my best recollection of the events and times with friends and family. Due to the limitations of my perspective as a child and young adult, I was compelled at times to create what I trusted was plausible and likely dialogue to bring the actual scenes to life. Until recent times, South Sudanese people did not keep track of birthdays— or celebrate them in any lavish way—so such dates and ages throughout the story are based on my best assumptions.

Shaded area would become the independent nation of South Sudan in 2011, with Juba its capital

SAUDI ARABIA

◎ SANA'A
Y E M E N

DJIBOUTI

…PIA

S O M A L I A

INDIAN · OCEAN

MOGADISHU ◎

MILES

0   100   200   300   400   500

GER'S FAMILY TREE

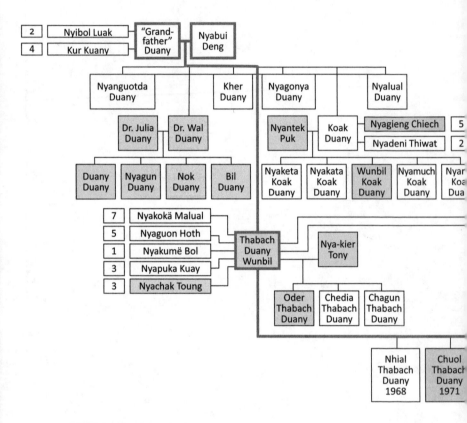

2	Nyibol Luak	
4	Kur Kuany	

"Grand-father" Duany — Nyabui Deng

Nyanguotda Duany — Kher Duany — Nyagonya Duany — Nyalual Duany

Dr. Julia Duany — Dr. Wal Duany

Nyantek Puk — Koak Duany — Nyagieng Chiech [5] — Nyadeni Thiwat [2]

Duany Duany — Nyagun Duany — Nok Duany — Bil Duany

Nyaketa Koak Duany — Nyakata Koak Duany — Wunbil Koak Duany — Nyamuch Koak Duany — Nyar Koa Dua

7	Nyakokä Malual
5	Nyaguon Hoth
1	Nyakumë Bol
3	Nyapuka Kuay
3	Nyachak Toung

Thabach Duany Wunbil — Nya-kier Tony

Oder Thabach Duany — Chedia Thabach Duany — Chagun Thabach Duany

Nhial Thabach Duany 1968 — Chuol Thabach Duany 1971

KEY

☐ Direct Ancestor

▨ Appears in Book

[1] Number of Children

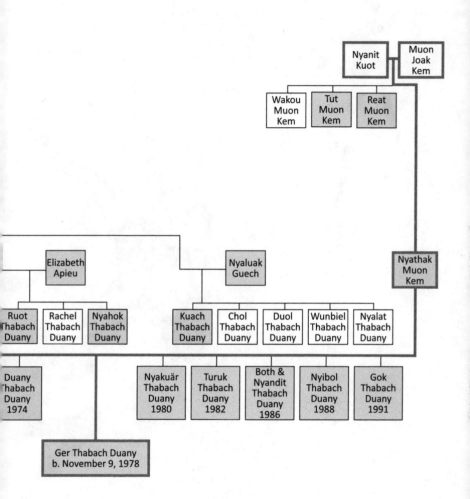

PART 1

BELONGING

I WAS ABOUT SIX YEARS old when I sat in the dirt clearing of Liet Village center in 1983 or '84, amid a few hundred other villagers, frozen in silence, watching my mother's youngest brother, Tut, lay his full six-foot, six-inch frame down in the dirt. The wind whooshed through the high grass, sorghum, maize, and tobacco on our subsistence farm, which surrounded our mud huts, and cattle lowed in the distance. Tut crossed his arms over his muscular chest and placed his shaved head inside a depression dug into the earth specially to catch the blood. He lay there without a trace of labored breathing or a single tremble while one of our village elders delivered a booming speech about courage, a man's responsibility to provide for his community, and his right to take wives.

ELDER 1: This young man will be marked into adulthood this morning. God protected him from many battles so that he might receive this honor in front of his elders and peers.

Another elder rose and gestured with long, graceful arms as he spoke.

ELDER 2: Today is a blessing. It is important in our culture to mark every Nuer man, so when the world looks upon him, they will know he is the bravest of all men and will protect his people at all costs. There have been many courageous warriors throughout history, each one a legend: Muon Kem Joak, Ger Pathot, and Buth Diu, who spearheaded the self-determination of southern Sudan. On this day, Tut will join their storied ranks.

A third elder, known for steady hands, pulled a ceremonial knife from its place among the coals of a small fire (where it was first sterilized). The lines on this elder's face deepened as he wiped the knife with a cloth, leaned over Tut's face, and frowned in concentration. The shadow of a hawk in flight flashed across the sunny clearing, and the elder cut a line all the way across the blank canvas of Tut's forehead.

Due to the knife's sharpness, the blood did not come right away. It was almost as if its edge hadn't even slid across his brow. Clean, precise, imperceptibly thin, like a paper cut. Then I saw a line, the line turned red, and after another second, the blood began to drip into Tut's ears. By the time it started gushing from the wound, the elder had already carved a second line below and begun a third, parallel to the first two. He didn't stop until he had carved six lines across the brow, and by then torrents flowed into Tut's eyes and all across his cheeks. The blood darkened the already-black earth beneath his crown and brightened Tut's dark complexion with a crimson sheen.

Of course I knew he was a living, breathing man, but while the cutting took place, Tut could have been obsidian, or the casket of a pharaoh, he was so perfectly still. Had Uncle Tut shown even the slightest twinge of pain during the ceremony, the entire assembly would have shuffled away in silent shame, but he had been the very embodiment of bravery, so the village exploded into a wild trill.

VILLAGERS: *Hulululu!*

I wasn't afraid at the sight of all that blood, for I knew this was only a ritual and Tut was not mortally wounded. My elders were there, my aunties, my uncles, my mother, and my father's other wives, and if they condoned this rite, I knew it was okay.

Having proven himself by receiving the cuts in silence, Tut stood, hands at his sides, eyes closed behind a curtain of blood. The cuts, which would heal into proud scars, bled out naturally as the elders led the newly initiated warrior into a hut where he would rest and recuperate.

Tut was actually too old to undergo this rite of passage and should have completed it when he hit puberty.

But he had recently returned to Liet from Sudan's Muslim-dominated north, eager to bond with his people and fight for the south in the second Sudanese civil war, which had begun that year. This was his way of proving his fealty to our village, our people, and our cause.

As soon as he entered the hut, men, women, and children alike jumped up and danced in the square, pounding their feet, throwing arms out, swiveling hips, and singing in celebration of this propitious initiation. I joined them, feeling the joy of the whole village in my bones.

At some point soon, village women would deliver food to Tut in grateful thanks for his dedication to the defense of the Nuer, our ethnic group. And eventually, after days or weeks—however long it took Tut to heal alone in the hut—he would finally emerge. And he would emerge a man.

While the villagers danced, I heard a powerful bovine bellow cut short as my uncle Reat leaned forward and, with a single stroke, sliced the throat of a favorite cow. The animal kneeled, its head drooped, and finally it collapsed on its side with a great thud. I nearly cried out when I saw its once-powerful horns resting on the ground like two useless sticks, but taking my cue from Tut's bravery, I held back my tears.

My father had warned me that a cow would be sacrificed as part of the ceremony, but still, when its blood gushed out and the majestic animal fell to its knees, my stomach turned sour, almost as if I were watching an auntie or uncle pass away. A cattle herder already, I had named each of my father's cows and knew their personalities by heart. I could identify which were easily led or rebellious, which were playful or slow-moving. Cows, for the Nuer people, are kin and currency: killing one is like losing a family member and lighting a wad of hundred-dollar bills on fire. But this significant occasion called for a sacrifice, a nod to the traditional animism that still colored our mostly Christian belief system.

My father did not require his sons to participate in the ritual scarification to which Tut had submitted, perhaps because it would brand us as villagers and declare inferior tribal status to Sudan's ruling elite, even more than our black skin already did. "Arabs" was what we called the northern Sudanese because they spoke Arabic; however, they weren't actually Arabs. They were a light-skinned African ethnic group that practiced Islam. Their side of this war was funded by allies in the Arab world, while Russia funded ours, indirectly, through communist Ethiopia. I'd grown up hearing stories about my older brother Oder, who was said to be a great soldier like my father, which had made my father immensely proud.

DAD: You boys should not participate in this serious initiation without full knowledge of what it means, do you understand?

Yes, I did understand the implications, as well as the honor of being declared a man, and I secretly wanted to receive the marks when I reached puberty.

Like Uncle Tut, I too had once lived in the northern-controlled area, and even attended preschool in the city of Malakal. But for our safety, my father set aside his business interests there and brought the family home again to this quiet village. Liet was nestled among the grasslands of rural Akobo County, in fertile Jonglei State, in the vast river valley of the Greater Upper Nile region of Sudan. Then the largest country on the African continent, Sudan was bordered by the Red Sea to the northeast, Egypt to the north, Chad to the west, and, to the south and east, six other countries professing varying degrees of friendship or hostility to the renewed fight of the southern Sudanese for equality under the repressive laws imposed by the government in the north.

Of course, during that day's ceremony, I knew nothing of such complex issues and faraway countries. I only knew that I felt whole, joyful, and safe in Liet and hoped never to leave our collection of mud huts set upon a swath of cleared land. I planned to forever herd cattle in the high grass that stretched to the horizon, dotted with termite mounds and stately, flat-topped acacia trees. In fact, the trees' inverted-triangle shape seemed to point deep into the grasslands as if to say, *Here is the spot where you belong, Nuer boy. Right here.*

THE HUNT

EACH DRY SEASON, MY FATHER would choose a camp in Upper Nile State for the entire family to travel to, based on which region seemed safest. That year's dry season, we drove the cattle to a vast grassland known as Luääl. There, every morning, a herd of antelope would come to drink, and our men would wake up before the dawn to hunt them. These were our few months to fatten ourselves up before returning to a meager diet of maize and sorghum, back in the village. We killed and ate as much meat as we possibly could in order to endure the long spell of scarcity, our continent's yearly reminder to be ever grateful for whatever the earth saw fit to provide.

Southern Sudanese people tend to be quite tall and lanky, and my uncle Reat, my mother's brother, was six feet nine, which is even taller than me. I thought he looked like a carved and sanded-smooth tree trunk. It was from him that I picked up an interest in keeping people and facts alive through storytelling. His tales were so animated and detailed, you felt you were inside them with whomever he was skillfully bringing to life with the sound of his voice, like a goddess of limitless fertility.

One evening, as my older brother Duany Thabach Duany (named after my grandfather), my cousin Wunbil (technically my stepbrother because my father had inherited his mother as a wife), and I prepared for bed, he came into our hut and spoke with authority.

UNCLE REAT: Boys, tomorrow morning you will learn how to be men.

DUANY: I am nine years old, Uncle. I'll be fighting in wars soon. Does that not already make me a man?

UNCLE REAT: Babies fight for milk. Girls fight over hair combs. Fighting does not prove one's manhood. Ger, do you know what makes a boy a man?

I was too embarrassed to say what I was thinking. I think Uncle Reat picked up on that.

UNCLE REAT: It's the hunt to feed your family. And you three boys will be accompanying the men on our quest tomorrow morning. So get a good night's rest.

Uncle Reat left, and we three jumped up and down, too excited to do anything but celebrate, until our mothers told us to *shh*. And then we lay on our cowhide rugs all night, dreaming with our eyes open about how strong and skill-ful we'd be, and of how many mouths we would feed with our countless kills, and of the fanfare with which we'd be showered when we returned, heroes of the hunt. Men.

My uncle arrived well before dawn to fetch us. After grabbing our spears and clubs, we joined the rest of the hunting party for a walk of about fifteen miles to a water-ing hole, where my uncle instructed us kids to crouch down with him in the tall grass. Other small groups of hunters crouched here and there in a vast, open land. As the sun rose, I watched the endlessly high grass wave in the breeze like fine fur. Soon the earth rumbled. I both heard the sound and felt the ground shake beneath my feet.

Uncle Reat tugged at my shoulder.

UNCLE REAT: Crouch lower, Ger. They're coming!

A moment later, hundreds of antelope galloped over the horizon, as one body. The brown mass of them moved closer and closer. I felt certain they would trample us, and I squirmed, feeling the urge to run.

UNCLE REAT: Sit still, son, and watch!

Just as the herd came close, a few young men in the hunting party popped up out of the grass and ran around among the animals, causing the herd to scatter in surprise and fear. At that point, Uncle Reat grabbed my arm, hard, and told me, Duany, and Wunbil to stand with him.

All the other hunters stood too, targeting the panicked antelope. Spears flew everywhere, and I heard the triumphant sound of *Hulululu!* filling the air.

UNCLE REAT: See that?

He pointed at one of the confused animals that were running toward us. I felt as terror-stricken as the beast, but my uncle's clear directives helped me focus.

UNCLE REAT: Steady. Stay still and steady. Wait until you can hear its breathing and smell its sweat.

With danger all around the animal, its only option was to use its impressive speed to reach safety miles away, charging forward and trampling whatever predator lay in its path.

I waited, watching the animal's body come nearer, its torso rippling, its hooves beating the ground with a ferocity matched in that moment by my heart. It ran with a determination that made it clear: only one of us was making it out of this encounter alive. The antelope was nearly upon us, and I hurled my spear with all my might. It caught the beast in the ribs.

The animal fell and my uncle crowed.

UNCLE REAT: *Hulululu!*

He was so proud of my accomplishment, yet I stood there dumbfounded. Then he called out.

UNCLE REAT: Name your favorite cow, Ger! Shout the name!

This is a traditional way to celebrate a kill, but my mouth went slack, my mind went blank, and suddenly I couldn't think of a single name of the hundred cows that I herded daily. The other villagers laughed at my shock until, finally, I thought of one.

ME: Nyang Mi GÉÉR, Nyang Mi GÉÉR!!

It was a bull full of gentleness, bravery, and intelligence, with hair and skin an astonishing patchwork of maroon, white, and gray, and long, creamy horns that had grown in two separate directions.

When I shouted it, everyone trilled their approval.

THE WARRIORS: *Hululululu!*

I couldn't believe I had done it. My hands hadn't shaken, nor had my knees trembled, though for the life of me I had no idea why my body had shown a bravery my mind hadn't felt.

The villagers of Liet thought people from the cities were soft and could not be brave or confident in the face of danger. My family had spent the first few years of my childhood in the city of Malakal, so I felt especially elated to prove them wrong that day.

UNCLE REAT: This boy is a hunter already!

We cut up the animal into parts, then packed it neatly in tree leaves and branches to protect the meat from flies. Once we returned to our village, Uncle Reat made a beeline for my mother, beaming as he delivered me and my antelope back to her cooking fire.

UNCLE REAT: One day, he will be a great warrior!

My mother was quiet but immensely proud of me, which was the best feeling in the world. Duany had not brought home the beast; I had. I was the breadwinner that day. She hugged me tight and I burst inside. She rubbed my head and murmured.

MUM: Tulu! Tulu! Tulu!

That was her special nickname for me. Though I was only around seven, that day I felt like a man—although, in every single way, I had a long ways to go.

LIFE LOST

DAD HAD A SMALL SHOP in town, where men gathered to talk about the latest news of the civil war. My father was a consummate businessman as well as a soldier, and his store had a corrugated zinc roof, a prosperous step up from the thatched roofs of most buildings. His first store had been destroyed by a lightning strike, about a year before Tut's initiation. The whole place went up in flames in a great flash of light and smoke, and I had to run out of there like everyone else. It took me a moment to stop crying and calm myself down enough to yell for help. But my father had been busy trying to save supplies, so he didn't come to my immediate aid. I essentially had to save myself and later wondered if that incident had made me a little bit more of a man, like Tut.

My dad soon rebuilt the shop, restored it as a social hub, and even began importing dry goods and beer from Malakal. Sometimes I liked to sit on the dirt floor and just listen to the words of the men, even though I didn't grasp their full weight.

Today they were talking about the first civil war and how the 1972 agreement that ended it, the Addis Ababa Accord, would not sustain the southern Sudanese.

DAD: This agreement was just a ploy by Arabs to plan another war in this land so that they could slit our throat like goats.

UNCLE: So you think they will use Sharia law to suppress us? And that Islam will spread all over East Africa?

DAD: Most certainly yes. The northern Sudanese know that East Africans will not resist their religion. Plus, East Africans are all about partying and drinking, and letting the white man turn their land into tourist attractions. So we have to rally Ethiopians. Not only are they good warriors, but with our interconnected history, they are also the most likely to come to our aid.

I nodded and looked back and forth among the men, acting like I understood grown-up talk but feeling inside like the confused, insignificant little kid I was.

I spent my days mostly wrestling with my brothers and cousins on the muddy banks of the lazy Akobo River.

We leaped through the tall grass and competed in rock-throwing, puddle splashing, footraces, and anything else that allowed a future warrior to prove his mettle. Of course, I also tended to my father's cattle, but they didn't need too much care during the warm, peaceful days of Akobo's wet season. Late one afternoon, I was sitting in our huge, round hut with Duany and Nyakuar, my little sister, chewing stalks of sugarcane while our mother stirred a pot of *wal wal*. From the sky, I heard something in the distance that called to mind a mad flock of huge birds beating their wings. I didn't know what the *flap-flap-flap* signified, but the look on my mother's face told me it was something more horrible than I could imagine. Mum, who was heavily pregnant, dropped the pot of sorghum porridge, grabbed up Nyakuar—setting her on a shoulder—and ran for the door.

MUM: Duany! Ger! Get to the forest as fast as you can!

We ran by Mum's side toward the cover of trees while several young village men crossed in front of us, racing to the precious cattle to herd them into the forest too. In the distance, the *rat-a-tat* of AK-47 fire sounded, and looking across the grassy plain that separated Liet from the next village, I saw flying machines hovering. Fire flashed from these helicopters, and flames leaped up from the village as grass-thatched roofs caught fire. It was only because Liet was attacked second that my family was saved.

By the time the helicopters reached us, Mum, Nyakuar,

Duany, and I, along with most of the other villagers, had hidden safely in the nearby forest. As the helicopters approached, I did not hear the familiar *rat-a-tat* of AK-47s, but rather a sequential snapping sound I would soon come to associate with something even more lethal: rocket-propelled grenades, or RPGs. Stragglers and stray cattle fell down dead, and walls of huts collapsed from the explosions. Then the helicopters headed toward the forest, despite the fact that the darkness of the jungle at dusk should have hidden us.

MUM: Run deeper into the jungle, boys. Now!

The helicopters got nearer and nearer. Suddenly Mum set little Nyakuar on the ground and leaped on top of Duany and me. She pulled us down into a puddle and rolled us in mud until the bright white school uniforms we had been wearing—souvenirs from our preschool in Malakal—were stained completely brown.

Mum was breathless as she spoke.

MUM: Your uniforms! Your white uniforms!

It was then that I realized the whiteness of the cloth had given away our position in the forest, making it easier for the helicopter pilots to chase and try to kill us. But now, with every inch of us coated in darkness, we blended into our nighttime surroundings like antelope on the grassy plains. The choppers had little choice but to head back to the village, where they dropped fire on a few more huts before leaving entirely.

I was only six or so at the time, so please forgive me for being terribly annoyed that my beautiful white uniform was ruined. I sulked over this loss as the villagers gathered in the forest that night. The elders discussed what everyone should do and decided that we would return to the village and bury our dead, but that since the enemy might return the following day, we should be back in the jungle when the sun came up.

We developed a routine of sleeping in our huts at night, then spending our days deep inside the jungle. In a claustro-phobic clearing, the women cooked our meals over small fires while we boys kept an eye on the cattle that wandered the woods. Living in the forest like that put us in grave danger, because the beasts there—like cheetahs, snakes, black scorpions, spiders, and huge bees—could have killed us just as easily as our armed enemy; thus, we stayed close together, finding safety in numbers. None of us wanted to make this our new life, but the elders, who had lived through the first Sudanese civil war, lectured us on how ruthless our opposition was.

ELDER 1: Do you gentlemen think our Sudan People's Liberation Army will be able to resist this oppressor from the north?

ELDER 2: Yes, but we must get a new partner who can supply weapons.

A CIVILIAN: I think SPLA will recruit more manpower during the dry season to launch more campaigns.

ELDER 1: I heard Egypt, Libya, Saudi Arabia, and Russia will be providing military assistance to the northern Sudanese.

ELDER 2: You children take heed: Our enemy is completely willing to kill civilians to achieve their means. You are precious to us, but mosquitoes to them—just pests whose only purpose is to help them find more efficient ways to exterminate you.

It had been ten days since the attack, and everyone agreed they hated living in the forest.

UNCLE REAT: It does not seem that the enemy is coming back. Maybe it's worth the risk to return home.

It did not take much to convince every last one of us to head back to Liet and resume our old lives. I said good-bye to my bug and beast neighbors and practically led the way as we trekked home, more nervous and excited now than afraid.

From that point forward, we had to keep one ear to the ground and one eye on the sky, as the notion of the civil war, with our village's fathers, husbands, and sons fighting, was no longer an abstraction. We knew now we were pawns in a very dangerous game, where our deaths were tallied up like currency.

LIKE FATHER, LIKE SON

SHORTLY AFTER THE ATTACK, DAD returned home with his platoon for a brief visit. From inside our hut, I watched him adjust the AK-47 on his shoulder and spit on the ground. Two men stood before him, clad like Dad in brown SPLA uniforms, as he gave them an order.

> DAD: Let us assess the area since we'll be spending some time in this village. We must be on high alert at all times and keep an ear out for when we will be ordered to join headquarters.
>
> SOLDIERS: Yes, Comrade Duany!

They saluted him and greeted my mother with a grunt as they walked away.

Dad placed his AK-47 in a corner and sat on a piece of cowhide. Mum handed him a wooden bowl into which she'd spooned some freshly cooked *kööb,* a special-occasion meal made from a type of African couscous mixed with butter and dried fish. He tasted the food without comment.

ME: Dad, why did those men call you "comrade"?

Luckily, my father was in the mood for answering questions.

DAD: We are all comrades in the great army. Those Arabs up north think they're better than us, but all people are equal—or will be, anyway—when we build New Sudan. You see, Ger, those Arabs are the ones that attacked you recently. They are our enemy.

I didn't fully understand, but I wanted to. So I risked his wrath at my stupidity.

ME: But I heard our enemy was called Anya Anya II.

Dad barked at me.

DAD: Yes, the Anya Anya II are also our enemy. But they hate the Arabs too, so in that respect they are our allies. However, they don't want the Great Society; instead, they want southern Sudan to secede from the north completely. That's why they fight us. But we will defeat them. Now, no more questions!

My dad's shifting emotional states always unsettled me. Mum once told me Dad had been less brusque, even kind, before the civil war, before my earliest memories, but the soldier's life had changed him. He now seemed to be preoccupied by the bigger, heavier matters of Sudan.

Anya Anya II and the SPLA were one and the same people, with different visions for our people's liberation. The SPLA, under the leadership of Dr. John Garang, believed in something called New Sudan, where all the diverse ethnic and religious groups of Sudan would coexist peacefully, national resources would be shared equitably, and representation in government would be proportionate. Anya Anya II, on the other hand, believed in the immediate separation of the principally Christian south (which was where I came from) from the predominantly Islamic north, with each of the two Sudans enjoying complete autonomy. It was an ideological divide of a people who were all pursuing equality and fairness, especially for minorities (Sudan's southerners, who were darker than the northerners, were considered a minority). It was a vision that would find a point of convergence decades later when the south became an independent state.

Anya Anya II fighters were predominantly from my Nuer ethnic group, but Dr. Garang was from the other large ethnic group, the Dinka. The Nuer and Dinka would come to have a long-lasting political rivalry that consigned the entire south Sudanese liberation movement and later the independent nation of South Sudan to a near-permanent state of internal strife. However, when Dr. Garang launched the SPLA, leaders within the Nuer community would overlook Anya Anya II and side with the SPLA. My father was one of those who stood by Dr. Garang from the word go, putting his shared, bigger national agenda ahead of any ethnic ties that might have led him to join his fellow Nuer tribesmen in Anya Anya II.

In 1983, with the offer of Soviet funds and a new impetus brought by the likes of Dr. Garang, my people took up arms once more against our oppressors. In between the civil wars, the various ethnic groups of the south had fought over individual rivalries, so it had been a long time since southern Sudan knew peace. Ideological conflicts emerged, and AK-47s became common household items to kids like me.

I was torn, trying to decide which path I wanted to take to prove I was a man. I wanted to receive a Nuer initiation into manhood, like Uncle Tut, but I also wanted to take up arms and fight for the SPLA, like Dad (though I didn't understand the war's complexities). My older brothers Oder and Chuol were already at an SPLA training camp in Bonga, Ethiopia, and I felt envious of them because they seemed to have joined the ranks of men. For the moment, Dad's AK-47, standing there in the corner, taller than I was, was off-limits to me. But to my childish way of thinking, shooting that gun, joining the SPLA, and attacking those who had attacked us were the highest goals to which I could aspire and would finally confirm my manhood in the eyes of my short-tempered, preoccupied dad.

WHAT IF?

BACK IN 1986, THE YEAR I turned seven (I think), my mother gave birth to twins so tiny they could each almost fit in a man's hand. The boy was named Both, and the girl, Nyandit. A year later, my younger sister Turuk died suddenly from an intestine infection and malaria. She was only two. Sorrow over her death haunted my mother, and it was compounded by another, almost graver loss—one she knew for sixteen years was coming but for which she could never, in her heart, be prepared.

Chuol left for Bonga a year or so after Oder had. Chuol was only fourteen, and somehow the fact that Mum had had more time getting to know these boys made the pain she felt at their absence almost physical—like she was an amputee, and they, her ghost limbs.

She had simply never expected any of her children to leave before they were fully formed, and not being able to see them grow into men and women was like being the victim of a violent theft. In Nuer culture, people don't show physical pain, but emotional pain is different. When we're happy, we dance and sing; when we're sad, we mourn; and when we're angry, we fight. Nothing is held inside, so witnessing the way my mother plodded when she fetched water, eyes downcast, without a spring in her step, I knew how badly this turn of events affected her.

She told fewer stories to us at night, and I missed hearing about how various animals that roamed the wild came to be the way they were. When I saw her once-bright eyes shining with tears while she swept the floor and did other simple tasks, I knew I had to try in every way possible to be of help to her. I dedicated myself not only to tending the cattle, but also to helping bring up the newborn twins, primarily by serving as a human baby carriage. I was seldom seen without one of them clinging to my back, although Mum also devised a small *dieny*—a traditional baby carrier made of a bundle of sticks—that the twins could ride in during our annual trek.

More importantly, I tried even harder to be for her everyone her heart had lost. It tears you apart inside, the inauthenticity of living as someone else. And just think— I had taken on the burden of four others (including my dad), and counting. Needless to say, as much as I wanted it to, that could not last forever. To be frank, it could not last for long.

There would be endless reports reaching my family about Oder's time in the army, and whenever this happened, there would be excitement all around me, with everyone going on and on about Oder this and Oder that. All I could rely on was an almost empty sense of nostalgia, feeling like I knew him, yet knowing that I hadn't spent enough time with Oder to speak about him with the sort of familiarity everyone else did.

My feelings about my brother centered mostly on a profound neediness—needing more conversations with him, more observations, more shadowboxing, more hugs. Less wondering about an enigma and more time with a boy who'd become a superhero to me. And isn't it always the case with heroes that their greatest sacrifice is time with their loved ones in exchange for fighting for the greater good? But what if what's good is unclear? What if neither side is actually on yours? What if having that hero away from home causes more harm to the family than help in resolving political conflicts? Yes, what if.

THE MESSENGER

FIGHTING HAD BECOME WIDESPREAD AND unpredictable during the wet season that year. One morning in July or August, as I brought the cattle out to graze on the fecund, almost neon, verdant grasses, a man dressed in *laawË or kuir,* a traditional piece of clothing tied across the body with a knot at one shoulder, approached. I had my favorite cow with me, which stopped its grazing to instead study the stranger with wide-set eyes.

STRANGE MAN: Are you a son of Thabach Duany?

I knew better than to just give up my identity to someone whose intentions I did not know or trust.

ME: I am a farmer and I am minding my business.

STRANGE MAN: You do resemble him. You have a lot of teeth.

By his reply, I knew he had been sent by my father with news of some kind: maybe a warning, maybe instructions, maybe word about a loved one. I would come to dread, in the ensuing years, the sight of a straight-faced man scarified with six lines across his forehead, floating across the horizon toward us, because it would often portend a deadly outcome.

This time, however, his sudden appearance was far more benign.

STRANGE MAN: Your mother is to take you, the twins, and Nyakuar to Diror Village in West Akobo. Your half brothers and sisters and their mums will not be far away, in Buong Village. Your father wants all four of his wives and his brother's wife, his seventeen children, and their cousins safe.

Without hesitation or debate, within two days we'd prepared maize, sorghum flour, and cashews, packed them up with not much else, and were on foot on the road to Diror, twenty miles away.

My father was very resourceful in finding ways and people to pass along messages and communicate with us. At the start of the dry season in 1986, he sent word with a different man that last year's camp, Luääl, was no longer safe because Anya Anya II was expected to attack.

The man found his way to our well-organized hut in

Diror, which was made of mud and wood and had a grass roof. My uncle Reat had built it alongside a huge cattle hut. My mother was taking out Nyakuar's hair so she could wash and rebraid it, and the smell of butter and milk from the *wal wal* and *kööb* in our outside kitchen hit my nose, causing my stomach to blurt out its approval.

There was a knock at the door, and Nyakuar and I raced to answer it, while the twins rolled around on the floor.

I beat Nyakuar to the door, but she pushed me back and opened it, revealing this new stranger on the other side. He didn't actually stop to speak to us, just strode right in, like he was a long-lost relative home in time for supper. He addressed my mother, Nyathak, who was called Nyamuon as a term of endearment.

NEW STRANGER: Mama Nyamuon? It is time. Your husband has summoned you to Bukteng. He is in the barracks of the temporary SPLA headquarters there. The whole family will reunite.

MUM: That is wonderful news! Did you hear, Ger? We finally get to be together again!

The energy on this trek was different from that of years past. I was buzzing on the outside, and inside my own head. What would it be like to be a family of twenty-plus people? We'd been separated for months, but now there'd be no end of children to play with—maybe even less responsibility since, among my father's four wives, there would be at least one free parent available to watch over the youngest kids. Even though I found the twins amusing, I'd be delighted to hand them off to somebody else to look after. Sometimes—not always, but sometimes—I just wanted time to be a kid myself.

Along the way, we ran into members of our extended family. Coming from the east and west, their herds of cattle joining with ours, they all walked north with us. We kids shouted, played, and ran like crazy through dry, cracked mudflats, brittle brown scrub grass, and, as we finally approached Bukteng, head-high green grasses that bent to and fro in the wind, like fingers beckoning us. As much as possible, we kept clear of dangerous jungles and confusing swamps, enjoying the safety of our numbers, yet always keeping our eyes out for lions and other carnivores that wouldn't hesitate to eat a human.

Gradually, the Duany extended-family group became complete as we trekked the hundred or more miles across Akobo into Upper Nile. The twins, Both and Nyandit, took turns riding on my back, and Nyakuar clambered along at my heels as I urged our sixty to seventy cattle ever forward. Our herd was rather ostentatious in its size, but my father was wealthy. And with all these kids, he would need that many cattle to successfully marry us all off.

ME: Wunbil! Come help! Kuach-Taar is so lazy, it's slowing us down!

My cousin ran over with his staff and poked at the lazy beast, which huffed and voiced its extreme disapproval at being forced to take a single step more.

As we entered camp, I noticed it looked well protected by plenty of SPLA soldiers. There was room enough for huts for all of us in a clearing beside the Nile. With the river running shallow at this time of year, I was hoping Nyandit would be less terrified of getting her bath, and I was looking forward to learning to spearfish. More than anything, I hoped I'd get another chance to kill an antelope out in the bush. This time, I felt sure I wouldn't be frightened.

The camp was partitioned into three sections—one for cattle, one for the SPLA, and a space for us, the families of SPLA fighters. The first order of business was to build the grass-thatched houses we'd stay in for three to four months.

Feeling like a grown-up, I immediately headed off to gather the longest, strongest blades of grass.

AUNT NYANTEK: Look at Ger! He's such a good boy, so reliable. Help Ger burn cow dung to repel flies and mosquitoes, Wunbil. You'd do well to follow his example.

Mum beamed: I was being recognized by another wife. I was happy to show Mum and everyone else that I was responsible and lovable—that I took care of my family. The best part about it, though? The quicker we set up, the sooner we'd be freed up to get into mischief.

Before we finished the last of the huts, built in a line parallel to the bank of the Nile, and before I could make my way toward the great river's shore to meet up with my siblings to play, I noticed Dad's dark brown eyes trained on me from the edge of the village. I took a deep breath and headed toward him, excited to see him but also full of trepidation.

My father seemed to approve of me, but I could never quite tell since worry always clouded his face. Back in Liet, Dad used to worry about business matters in addition to the war, but here, in this SPLA camp, his brow looked even more furrowed and his AK-47 never left his shoulder, not even while he slept.

I waited for him to speak first, as that was the polite way of greeting one's elders.

DAD: Ger, you are bigger than I remember.

Did he mean taller or fatter? Maybe a bit of both.

DAD: Have you been taking care of your mother?

ME: Yes, Dad. I am a man in our house and I help Mum with the chores and the twins.

DAD: You are still a boy, Ger, but you are growing up well.

ME: I have killed my first antelope.

Dad let out a noise that sounded like he was both gasping and sucking his teeth. I believe that was his way of telling me he was glad about my progress, but that I would have to kill more than a single antelope to be the kind of man he expected his sons to become. I eyed his AK-47 and wondered when I could shoot a gun like that. For then I surely could take down anything or anyone. Like my brother Oder, I would then have earned my dad's undying respect.

HOME

WE HADN'T EVEN BEEN IN Bukteng for a month when I awoke just before dawn to the rhythmic *rat-a-tat* of AK-47s and the *snap-snap-snap* of RPGs, followed by explosions and the sound of women and children screaming. I ran outside and saw in the distance that the barracks, where Dad bunked, were the epicenter of a ground attack. We had thought the SPLA would keep us safe here, but as it turned out, the army's presence actually attracted enemies. Anya Anya II rebels had surprisingly joined forces with soldiers of the government in the northern city of Khartoum, the capital of Sudan, to wage a massive assault against their common enemy, the SPLA.

The attackers descended upon us from a place of strategic advantage, attempting to force the entire population of our village into the Nile. We were trapped. Either we were going to die of gunshots, or we'd have to escape into the river, where the soldiers would still pursue us.

My dad and the entire SPLA were almost immediately outgunned. Why their spies did not know of or alert anyone to the ambush, I cannot say. Regardless, my family and I—all of the civilians, actually—were now on the run, and on our own.

Mum was visibly afraid, yet acted as though she'd rehearsed for this situation a thousand times over. She mounted one twin on each shoulder, then whispered to me.

MUM: Take Nyakuar's hand and do not let go for anything.

I grabbed my sister's left hand—in her right, she clutched her security blanket—and we dashed away from the gunfire, along with other fleeing villagers. Wherever bullets kissed the earth, puffs of dirt leaped from the ground all around us; it was as though we were in some kind of magic act where we'd vanish into thin air by the time the dust settled.

This time there was no forest nearby to hide within, so we did as our attackers had hoped and ran toward the Nile. The river was low, and its currents were relatively weak, but there were some sections that remained very deep. There was long grass along its banks, and some of the escapees tried to hide in it. But our attackers shot everywhere indiscriminately, in hot pursuit, flattening the SPLA camp, then shooting into the water and grass and across the river, using heavy artillery.

Charging through the high grass and splashing right into the knee-high river in the predawn darkness, I looked back momentarily and could see the piercing eyes of an enemy soldier as he fired in my direction. Quite frankly, I have no explanation for why I did not die that day . . . or any of the innumerable other days I've stared right in the face of death.

The spray of bullets and people charging through the obsidian-blue liquid reminded me of frenzied fish spawning or crocodiles thrashing their prey about. Nyakuar's wet blanket was slowing us down, and I wanted to yank it out of her hand. This was life or death, and none of the other villagers carried anything at all, except for their injured family members, and sometimes their dead. But if the blanket was the difference between a slower but focused child and a scattered, screaming one, letting her keep it was the better choice.

After slogging through the river for what felt like an eternity, we made it to the opposite bank and again ran through more high grass. We could still hear the gunfire on the other side of the Nile, but at this distance, we were safe.

To my surprise, Mum set us kids beside a termite mound and ran back the way we had come. I watched her flipping over dead bodies on the riverbank and questioning the living.

MUM: Have you seen my husband, Thabach Duany? Have you seen my husband?

People were too busy trying to reunite with their own loved ones to pay any real attention to her. I couldn't believe how much she had lost in the past two years. I did not know if her pure, beautiful heart could take another loss, even with three of her children still with her, needing her. Loving her.

Mum trudged back over, willing the tears back inside her head. But I was strong, I thought. I knew what to say to make her—and myself—feel better.

> ME: Dad is a soldier. He knows how to fight, how to hide, and how to ambush them right back. He would not have retreated with us. He would have led his soldiers to safety.

> MUM: Oh, Ger. Your father had all his family in one place. For a moment, our village felt like home. What devastating loss he must feel.

I knew she was speaking of her own loss too.

I figured Mum must have been awfully in love to have raced back to the riverbank in search of a man who could not have been there. What she'd done made no sense. But then again, neither love nor war ever does.

Along with other survivors, we watched the sun begin to color our world with broad brushstrokes while enemy soldiers across the river overran Bukteng. The SPLA had lost the fight, which meant we had lost our cattle—our livelihood—as well.

This battle felt different from the helicopter assault in Liet. It was one thing to be shot at from high up in the sky, but to look into the eyes of the enemy running down our streets, walking into our huts, that was something else entirely. I began to doubt, for the first time, that a soldier's life was for me.

At nightfall, people clustered into little groups, sitting, talking of the attack and the escape, trying to figure out who was dead and who was alive. We slept in the open air, both for lack of accommodation and to be able to spot the enemy were they to pursue us that far across the Nile.

The sun came out the following morning, and it was unanimously agreed that it was time to keep moving. Mum gathered her children together.

MUM: We had better get out of here before those soldiers find us.

I could hear exhaustion and high-pitched fear in her voice. Making another long and dangerous trek—before the blisters on our feet from the previous long journey had even healed—was the last thing she wanted to do.

ME: Can we walk home to Liet?

MUM: No, not in the dry season. Nothing grows. We'll only starve there.

I didn't know in which direction we were going, but because my mother had been through a civil war before, she knew where we had to head in search of safety. Then I asked her in a small voice what I'd really been wondering since we'd fled.

ME: Is Dad okay?

MUM: I don't know, son. All we can do is find a friendly village to stay in and try to send word to him that we're alive. Perhaps we'll hear back. I hope so.

Underneath her statement was our mutual concern—that we might not hear back because Dad might not have made it.

ME: Perhaps he is gone for good, like Uncle Machiel?

My father's younger brother was brought up around my mother from the time he was a little boy. He went to Khartoum as a teenager, intending to get an education. Over time, many uncles were sent to find him and convince him to visit Akobo, but it was a daunting task. Sometimes no one could find him for years. Many considered him a lost cause; he had no interest in returning to southern Sudan. He was a ghost uncle to me, which must've been what upset my mother.

MUM: Your father is in no way like his brother. He is steadfast. He is brave. And he always comes back.

Finding a friendly village to take us in was going to be no easy task, as we were strangers in the region, and some villages were loyal to the SPLA, while others were pro–Anya Anya II. My father was well-known as an SPLA first lieutenant (first lieutenant is a single star in military rank), so while one village would welcome us Duanys with open arms, if we walked into the wrong one . . .

The sun now sat atop the horizon, an orb of blinding white gold, revealing endless grassy plains on our side of the river. Other villagers dispersed in different directions, obviously scared and confused. I lifted Both onto my back, and he clung to my neck out of habit. I liked the feeling of his tiny, warm body against mine. I pointed to a tree in the distance.

ME: Should we walk toward that?

MUM: No.

She shielded her eyes from the morning's glare.

MUM: We'll walk toward the rising sun. That way lies Ethiopia, our ally.

A cloth wrapped around my mother's hips was the only piece of clothing among us. We had no food, no cattle, nothing but each other. Mum placed Nyandit on her shoulder, Nyakuar took my hand in hers—infuriating, filthy blanket glued inside her other one—and we walked.

This was the day our lives as Sudanese villagers ended. We were now refugees.

THE TREK

WE WALKED TOWARD ETHIOPIA, EVERYONE growing frail. I couldn't keep count of the days and nights we traveled through villages and across unsettled, untamed lands. There was little to eat, but we survived on the sheer generosity of villagers through whose territory we passed.

We came upon one such village, called Macbany, on the outskirts of historical Thiayjak Town. We were famished, tired, and dirty. But the amazing thing was, we were not treated like the unwanted homeless people you often come across in Western countries. We were not shunned or ignored. No one pretended we didn't exist. Instead, it was like we were marathoners huffing and puffing through the seventeenth mile. People lined up along the bank of the beautiful White Nile River, and they offered us cow's milk, handfuls of catfish, and, sometimes, a place to rest our heads at night. There was a strange man in his sixties, with a few teeth missing, who went by the name Gatnoor Kombör.

GATNOOR: Where are you headed? Why have you walked so long your feet are both raw and callused?

MUM: We were caught in the battle at Bukteng.

GATNOOR: Oh, yes, I heard many civilians lost their livestock.

MUM: And we were run out of our summer camps.

GATNOOR: There was an intense fight here in Thiayjak too. Some of us were able to come back, but I sent many of my children to the Ethiopian refugee camp in Itang.

MUM: We are headed that way ourselves.

GATNOOR: You might no longer have a village, but you are not without a home. As long as you have family, home can never be far away, and my doors are open to you.

My Nuer people lived on both sides of the Sudan-Ethiopia border, which made it safe for us to cross into Ethiopia, despite the 1894 colonial demarcation that split communities and gave them different nationalities. Older folk had always spoken about the camp at Itang, where the United Nations helped people, where there was food and no gunshots, and—the most fascinating part—where kids could enroll in school and receive an education and—get this—not be taught in Arabic, as they were in Sudan. But I did not believe such a place existed, given the realities of my childhood.

Word was that the soldiers from Anya Anya II were pursuing us from a distance, seeking out SPLA soldiers suspected of hiding within the civilian population. Some of the soldiers who had managed to escape the attack at Bukteng hid within the herds of cattle with which we were walking, so there was an ever-present risk of infiltration, a permanent fear of the enemy within.

At one point, I did what I knew I shouldn't and asked my mum about Oder.

ME: Mum, do you believe Oder is alive?

MUM: Shh, Ger. You are never to speak of those we are missing. We will eventually hear one way or another. Do not tempt fate. And do not open wounds.

In order to survive psychologically, you had to either push the people out of your mind or assume they were dead if you hadn't seen them for a long time. Imagine having to believe your loved one was dead in order to live yourself.

Once on Ethiopian territory, we got to a place called Bilpam, which was a famous SPLA training ground set up with the Ethiopian Communist Party under Mengistu Haile Mariam, who was a strong supporter of the southern Sudanese liberation struggle. Civilians passing by the huge encampment waved at the soldiers. The SPLA at Bilpam was in effect our people's government-in-waiting, and the sense of respect for it was palpable.

This area of Ethiopia was seen as part of Sudan, separated by a porous border. Bilpam was predominantly occupied by people from southern Sudan, who moved fluidly between the two nations. To some, changing nationality was like swapping clothes, and I too felt like an Ethiopian once I crossed the border, since there was no physical difference between myself and the people I met there. They were tall and dark like those of us coming from Sudan.

Everyone around the SPLA, including little kids like me, knew that Bilpam was the place where the guns came from. Anyone who joined the SPLA rebellion had to go to Bilpam for training. The irony was that Anya Anya II was the originator of the Bilpam operation in 1978, but they had been kicked out by the SPLA under Dr. Garang through what some considered unsavory means.

We passed Bilpam just after the crack of dawn, and we arrived at midday at another significant location in the history of my people's struggle: the Itang refugee camp.

The sun was hot over our heads. To my probing eyes, the place was uncharacteristically green and beautiful, located on the banks of the Baro River, which flowed into the White Nile. Even when people fled in times of war, we tried to move along the banks of rivers, since our lives were dependent on water for ourselves and our cattle.

For the first time in my life, I saw in one area a large, diverse group of people with different languages. Some came from as far as central Sudan—the Nuba Mountains, the Blue Nile, and Darfur. The fact that all of them were from Sudan made me realize how huge my country was, and how different its inhabitants were from one another, even though, united in our crisis, we all spoke Arabic.

I was tempted to make a new friend among the thousands of people crowded together in our new surroundings. But it was just so overwhelming. There were so many stranded kids to choose from, and besides, my mother kept me and my siblings close to her side. She'd "lost" sons and her husband to war thus far. She was not about to lose another child, least of all in a crowd.

EXTENDED FRIENDS, EXTENDED FAMILY

WE REGISTERED AT A UNITED NATIONS office, where they took details of our family. As we headed out, my mother ushered us quickly toward Tielul I, a division of the camp, where my stepmother Elizabeth (my father's second wife) was to be our host and guardian. She had been there since our family had gotten split up in Luääl and had been elected to the head office in her section of Tielul I.

I recognized Elizabeth right away. She had already established a home here and welcomed us with open arms.

ELIZABETH: Nyathak, I will make sure to write a letter this week so that you all can secure your ration cards.

MUM: I heard the local director of the United Nations failed many families in that regard.

48

ELIZABETH: I will have my letter inside his office before morning.

MUM: Thank you, mother of our children. We are lucky, Ger. Oftentimes when you lose one family member, another one pops up at just the right time.

Elizabeth was an Anyuak from Sudan and had lived in Itang in the 1970s during the civil war. She was a well-known leader among the Sudanese within the camp and welcomed all refugees. She was educated and outspoken, and people looked up to her. Possibly thanks to her clout, my family received a larger portion of food than we anticipated.

Elizabeth's son, my elder brother Ruot, had escaped to Khartoum, where he went to school before proceeding to Egypt. He would go to America in 1989. In 1986, her daughter had been taken from Bilpam to Cuba, where the SPLA sent young Sudanese refugees to get a military or other specialized education. Many ten-to-thirteen-year-olds hoped for the opportunity to go to Cuba, since we all believed life would be better there. And Elizabeth had happy news for us.

ELIZABETH: Oder is in Cuba as well. Safe, though injured. He was shot—got a broken collarbone. Now he is recuperating. Such a brave young man.

My mum took in the news quietly. While the twins remained oblivious to any of the trauma she internalized, I, on the other hand, let out a scream. Oder was safe, perhaps getting an education, maybe never having to fight again. The family was now closer together, with wives receiving news of their children, even as the wars had kept us apart. Maybe the tides were turning for us.

A SMALL TASTE OF EDUCATION

I COULDN'T SLEEP. NOT BECAUSE we lay on the ground behind a fence on blankets we'd been given by the United Nations refugee agency, UNHCR, but because in the morning, I was going to enroll in school.

I arose before everyone else and woke up my sister Nyakuar and my cousins.

ME: We are going to school. We will be together with a lot of boys and girls. So it is better we wash our faces so that we can look presentable like city people.

NYAKUAR: Yes, it is true. We have to stick together to protect ourselves.

We dressed quickly and headed out without a bite to eat. First, we had to gather at an assembly point, where a group of SPLA soldiers, moonlighting as volunteer teachers and receiving a small salary from the Ethiopian Orthodox Church, led us kids in a mock military parade. We marched for more than an hour in a grand display, singing the Sudanese national anthem, which was the SPLA's way of indoctrinating even the youngest children into their ideology. This would happen every morning, rain or shine.

STUDENTS (SINGING IN BOTH NUER AND DINKA): *Sudan our country, Sudan our country, Sudan our country, Sudan our country, we are, we are forever!*

Then came the main event. There was no building yet, so class was held in the shade under a tree. The truth is, I had never been to a proper school, so I had nothing to compare it to.

Each of us had to get innovative and make a clearing on the sand using our feet and hands. There were no books, pens, or other school supplies, so we used the flat, soft surface on the ground as a page on which to scribble the alphabet with branches or our fingers, and no one dared mess up another's clearing. This fleeting opportunity for formal learning was too precious to most of us.

I met a little Nuer boy named Moses Chot, and he became a friend of mine. He was always playful and giggling, with the physical strength of an old man. During our break, we spent a lot of time kicking around a soccer ball made out of rubbish—a sock stuffed with plastic bags, ripped-up clothes, and paper.

MOSES: My uncle adopted me when I was four, because my family was burned in their hut right before the civil war broke out.

ME: I am lucky my father and brothers are still alive. Though I guess fear unites us all.

Friendships mounted—some that would last a lifetime, others cut short.

Peter Gatkuoth was three years older than me, had big lips and unusually light hair. Not a minute went by without him horsing around, trying to turn every little thing into a joke. My other lifelong friend, Jangjuol Biel Jangjuol, was a lot like me: young but forced to be grown-up by circumstance. Though he wasn't as tall and physically strong as most of us, whenever he wanted to achieve something—anything—nothing would get in his way.

After school, around two or three each day, I tended to my precious cattle. Sometime between marching in mock military parades, exercising, and going to the cattle camp, I received one daily meal and a small taste of education.

The refugee camp was meant to be free from arms, but the SPLA had infiltrated it and even set up a secret armory where guns and uniforms were hidden. The camp was always under SPLA protection whenever the UN officials were not around. Tens of SPLA soldiers would move around with their guns, dressed in their uniforms. But the moment the UN staffers reappeared, the guns and uniforms vanished instantly. It was an open secret among the Sudanese. The camp was viewed as an ideal recruiting ground for the SPLA. It was generally peaceful, but sometimes fighting broke out between the Ethiopians and Sudanese. Everyone would be armed, and deaths would occur. I first learned there that refugee camps were not necessarily the safest of places.

My favorite teacher was Deng Alier. He wore glasses with clear frames and taught us arithmetic. He was gentle, with a high-pitched voice. A lovely man and a great teacher, he liked me and encouraged my inquisitiveness.

DENG ALIER: Ger, you will have a future when New Sudan's vision is realized.

Mr. Deng and I did not speak after the Ethiopian civil war. I do not know if he survived.

Some of our teachers, like Simon Duol, had fought on the front lines and had missing limbs and other visible injuries.

SIMON: *E* and *a* together sound like the long *e*, as in "bean," "dream," and "blue jeans."

ME: Did you ever wear any?

SIMON: Please raise your hand before speaking. And did I wear what, Ger?

ME: Blue jeans.

SIMON: Once or twice.

I realized quickly that was kind of a silly thing to latch onto, but I was just so excited to learn everything I could about where I was and where I might go one day.

ME: How did you learn to type on a typewriter before you knew the English alphabet?

SIMON: It is about daily practice.

ME: What does it take to learn this typewriter thing?

SIMON: Keep observing me and one day you will be able to do it.

A good number of our teachers had been educated in Sudan before the war broke out. Against their will, some had to cut their studies short and undergo military training at the SPLA camps in Bonga and Bilpam before being deployed to the front lines in liberated areas like Nasir, Torit, and Bentiu. They showed unmatched commitment in teaching us, living by an unwritten SPLA rule that required more of all its combatants. Beyond just being a fighter, every member of the movement was expected to give back to the community, one way or another, by volunteering either their time or their skills. One such example was Peter Yak Jany, a volunteer teacher at our makeshift school, who discussed the difference between the South Sudan Liberation Movement and the Sudan People's Liberation Movement. He always preached that we must appreciate and embrace self-determination. He loathed New Sudan's vision of everyone coexisting and sharing in governance, and he was not a huge supporter of the Sudan People's Liberation Army (SPLA) because he thought its sole purpose was to benefit Dr. Garang and saw its leaders as hijackers of the people's movement. We called him "professor" because of his sharp intellect. He inspired a lot of young Sudanese refugees to seek an education, and was a big influence on my friend Lual Nyang, who was the best English speaker of my generation at the refugee camp.

Eventually, the UN and the Orthodox Church built a school, made of bricks, concrete, and rough zinc, which is when we were grouped according to age. We learned with kids from all over Sudan. Our fathers, for the most part, were SPLA soldiers. We were a mixture of boys and girls, young and old. None of us had been to formal school before.

BACK FROM THE DEAD

ITANG BROUGHT US MUCH-NEEDED STABILITY, a respite from our constant movement, but it was also very crowded. Hundreds of thousands of displaced people lived in its tents and mud huts, since everyone escaping Sudan had to pass through the camp whether they ended up in Egypt, Cuba, or America. The UN provided us with rice and beans, but in order to cook, women ventured deep into the forest, far away from the camp, in search of wood to fuel our traditional fires, made with three large stones upon which clay cooking pots were set.

During these trips to the forest, women risked assault from soldiers—some of whom were prone to rape them. I worried about my mother and aunts, hoping that someday I would become a great warrior and protect them. Hygiene was also a huge problem. I saw the most dead bodies I had ever seen in my life at Itang, where the graves were shallow.

The water wasn't clean, and cholera was prevalent since people drank from the river where they swam.

My last sister, Nyibol, was born in 1988 in the camp and succumbed to the flu at one year old. Another loss for my mother. Another death. Sometimes I'd wonder how a parent—especially my mum—found the will to wake up each day from dreams about the children she'd lost. What was in her spirit that convinced her that fighting for survival might still be worth it? A lot of children died in Itang.

One afternoon, as Nyakuar and I entered our hut after our lessons, we stumbled upon a soldier speaking with our mother. Mum turned to us with watery eyes, so I feared the worst.

MUM: It's your father, children.

I stopped breathing.

MUM: We have just received word he is alive!

I reanimated right then and embraced my sister, who was not much of a hugger and therefore tried to shake me off. But she was filled with joy too and let me hold her longer than she normally would. I had many questions.

ME: Where is he now? When will we see him? Does he have a message for me to decode?

Mum was more patient with me now that she knew Dad was safe, so she tolerated my questions and left the shushing up to the soldier messenger. He was not stingy with it.

After that day, I kept my ear to the ground and learned through eavesdropping on the conversations Elizabeth and my mother held in hushed tones that my dad was probably in hiding, occasionally showing up in Itang in the dead of night to check on my mothers. I also learned that Dad had been in charge of our movement the entire time on our journey from Bukteng to Itang. He'd been sending messages through intermediaries, who gave my mother directions for getting into Ethiopia safely.

Dad was a prominent target for his Anya Anya II tribesmen since he had originally joined them in fighting for the secession of the south from Sudan. He later deserted and joined Dr. Garang's SPLA, buying into the vision of a new, united Sudan, New Sudan. Anya Anya II was eternally hunting my father down, a man whom they saw as a traitor to their separatist cause.

MUM: I believe Anya Anya II spies infiltrated the caravan we traveled in here.

ELIZABETH: It is almost a certainty. And they would have killed him had he shown up.

MUM: If they followed us here, they are likely still among us. We cannot let anyone learn we know he is alive . . . or anything else.

My mothers said one of the main leaders of Anya Anya II, Bidit Deng, had been my dad's closest friend.

ELIZABETH: Even though Bidit is his mortal enemy, he was his friend first.

MUM: Bidit led the attack on Bukteng! Yet he is the one who told him Anya Anya II was looking for him. I suppose if Anya Anya II has spies, it's only fair we have them too.

I sensed that my dad was somewhere not too far away, possibly hiding in the nearby bush. He seemed omnipresent, running the show although we couldn't see him physically. There was consensus among my mothers that if Anya Anya II fighters got my family and took us hostage, they would be using us as bait to get to him.

The other thing my mothers spoke about at night was their wish to have us eventually go to Cuba to get a better education, like my brother Oder had done.

I had grown up hearing stories about Oder and Chuol, the warriors of the family, and had always wondered what it would feel like to be around these two young soldiers with whom I shared a bloodline, who remained remote ideas inside my head. Then one evening, out of the blue, a young man showed up at our family home in Itang. He came and sat under a tree, not speaking to anyone. I had absolutely no idea who he was. My mother approached him.

MUM: Young man, who are you?

The person looked up.

YOUNG MAN: I am your son Oder.

Everyone got hysterical. Everyone, including myself and my little brothers and sisters, started crying, embracing him. No one had imagined they would see him alive again, at least not that soon. My mother was especially overcome with emotion. It had been four or so years since Oder had left home to join the army. And now he was back. And I knew my father was somewhere nearby too.

There wasn't much else I could have wished for then. My heroes—the men I knew least but dreamed of becoming— were back in my world. I felt more whole than I had in years. But something gnawed at the back of my mind—it's one thing to know intellectually that your heroes are out there alive, fighting, performing feats historians will one day write about. It's another to have that flesh and blood before you. It all becomes real again. Thus, on the arm of joy, escorting it into your heart, is fear—fear that this is all temporary and, like life itself, could all be extinguished in an instant.

BROTHERS

ODER WAS THE BIGGEST INFLUENCE in my life growing up, just from hearing stories about him, but now I could hear, and see, and embellish stories of him in the flesh.

After a feast celebrating his return, Oder took me aside. For so long I had been holding down the position of the eldest boy in the house, so in this moment he felt he should convey to me some truths the eldest boy should know.

ODER: I know you heard me say I was her son, but your mother, Nyamuon, is not my biological mother, Ger.

I laughed. I knew of Oder's great strength and fighting skill, but his reputation was also of a jokester.

ODER: I am not kidding with you. I am not your full brother. We are halves.

He explained he was the only child from Nyakier, my father's first wife. Elizabeth was my father's second wife, and my mother was the third. His mother had divorced my father when Oder was still a little baby. And because his mother had a tough personality like my father, whenever they fought, she wouldn't relent. This was how she eventually decided to give the baby Oder to my father, who was fighting in the bush, and walk away.

ODER: This was during the original Anya-Anya rebellion, and Dad was moving from village to village. Apparently, our father struggled with baby me. So he needed another wife, and she ended up being our stepmother Elizabeth. Funny thing is, Elizabeth had an equally strong personality and wouldn't take Father's military dictatorial tendencies lying down either.

ME: Dad can be gruff.

The pain of being yelled at stabbed at my heart a little as I said this, but I patched over it with the respect I had for him as a warrior.

ODER: Our— Your mother had been orphaned at age twelve and had to take care of her little brothers and sisters, much like you do, Ger. One day our father passed through her family home and watched this twelve-year-old tend to her siblings and run the home.

ME: She ran the house at twelve?

ODER: She did. So you need to step up your game. She was fetching water, making food, and being all grown-up, which impressed Dad. He hinted to her extended family that he was interested in marrying her in the future and gave them some heads of cattle.

ME: Just the heads?

ODER: No! That is an expression. You know how valuable cows are—four hundred dollars each! Five hundred for a bull! And then Dad gave me to your mum so he could return to fighting. Your mother raised me. She is the mother I know and is my real mum. So, yes, I was telling her the truth when I said I was her son. But the truth is always complicated.

I was shocked to learn Oder and I were not full siblings—I wanted every piece of me to be just like him. But the truth is, it all made sense. He was wide and stocky, an acacia, while I and my full siblings were long and slim like mahogany. But it didn't matter. In a polygamous society like ours, where we have numerous brothers and sisters from one dad and many mothers, we value our relationships with each other until the end of time.

ODER: I hope you know this doesn't change a thing about us being brothers. Blood is thicker than water. But brotherhood is thicker than blood.

I thought about that. About the blood that ran down Uncle Tut's face as he vowed to fight for his people. About the bloodshed I'd seen all around me as friends, like my dad and Bidit Deng, and even family fought one another. And then about the people Oder and my father fought beside, despite most of them being a different ethnicity. My father and brother had chosen a family of fighters—brethren over kin. That made Oder even more special to me—for I was choosing him as my brother. And that love was thicker than blood or water or any other element known to man.

ORDER IN THE CAMP

MY OLDER BROTHER'S NAME, ODER, means "order"; my father named him after a guerrilla leader from his battalion in the 1960s and '70s. Given that, his path in life—to become a soldier like my father and also to be the one to order me around all the time—seemed preordained.

Oder taught me how to bathe myself thoroughly; he was not impressed by how the village kids in Itang cleaned themselves.

> **ODER:** Wash your testicles, penis, and bum thoroughly, Ger. There is no reason for people with access to water to be nasty.

I laughed out loud, but he was serious. He watched over me and was disgusted when I, for lack of a better term, half-assed it.

ODER: Get back in there and do it right. This is no laughing matter.

Maybe he found it a little funny, but he didn't let on. It was more important to him that I showed some self-respect and maintained the dignity of our family. And I could at least do that by making sure my hygiene was on point.

Oder was like a father to me, in that he taught me everything he knew and wanted better for me. Each evening, he took me to watch him play with a group of young Ethiopian men in an organized soccer game. He might have been one of the younger guys on the field, but Oder was aggressive, fast, and a great midfielder, plowing through defenders and assisting in countless goals. I guess you could say Oder fulfilled his duty countless times over; he continually showed me the way and inspired me to play soccer throughout my time in refugee camps.

When I wasn't kicking around a ball with Oder, Lual Nyang was my go-to guy. He owned a real soccer ball everyone wanted to play with, and you had to be in Lual's good graces for him to pick you to join in. Kids would follow Lual for hours on end, and every time he put his soccer ball on the ground, there would be a stampede, as everyone wanted to kick it. At times, this would make Lual angry and he would take the ball away, fearing it would get ripped.

Lual was a little older than me, restrained and philosophical, with long, girlish eyelashes and a frame so small and wiry it annoyed him greatly. Lual had spent more time in Itang than most of us, and was the only one who spoke what was considered proper English. Even Deng Alier thought of him as one of the brightest kids, which was hard to hear coming from the mouth of my favorite teacher.

Oder also taught me the proper way to breathe when I swam.

ODER: Like this. Turn your head to the side and take a breath in. Don't lift your head above the water; that stops you in your tracks and you will start to panic.

Sometimes I would pretend to be worse at swimming than I was and fake-drown, just to get on Oder's nerves. I was very successful at that.

And then there was the day I boxed him one time too many. I bapped him on the arm, then on the knee, then on the shoulder, trying to rile him up. That was my job as the little brother—to annoy the bigger ones. But this time I was met with a blow I never saw coming.

ODER: *Ghehii!*

Right to the gut. I felt like I'd been blown back by a rocket launcher. Lying flat on my back, I opened my eyes to see the stark blue sky, so clear and monochrome that I was not certain if I'd gone blind—until Oder stepped into my field of vision and offered me his hand to help me up.

ODER: Do not start a war you cannot finish, Ger.

But I was not interested in lectures or life lessons—now I just wanted to know how to hit like that!

ME: Teach me! Teach me that!

Oder told me he had been practicing Shotokan karate katas.

ODER: You became my test subject to see if it really works. I'm happy to report it does.

ME: Can I try it on you?

ODER: If you're going to do something, do it. Study it, then apply it, but not until you've mastered it. You, little brother, have a lot more learning to do.

Oder told me the importance of discipline. Needless to say, after that day, I sought out anyone at Itang who could teach me karate. The more I could do like Oder, the more I could be like him, and the closer I felt to him. He was just the coolest person ever. Eventually, I made a friend named Garang Barjok, who got selected along with me to train for karate in the camp. He loved sparring on the riverbank, which helped keep those moments of duking it out with Oder alive in the back of my mind. Garang was rugged, with slick black hair set atop a rectangular, chiseled face, and his perfect white teeth gleamed out from his dark gums when he smiled or laughed—whenever he threw me to the ground.

> ODER: If you become great in fighting, you can't use those skills on just anyone. Be wise, judicious, and fair. Know when it's time to walk away—when your enemy is beaten, be gracious, not a bully.

I often think back on those words, and how much Oder knew, even just as a teenager. Had I followed his advice, it might have saved me some heartache later. Then again, there was so much suffering to come, it was hard to keep straight in my head which words of wisdom to apply when.

CHRISTMAS

I NEVER GOT TO SPEND as much time as I wished I had with my brother Oder. My earliest memory of him was during the Christmas season sometime in the early 1980s.

We all gathered at the Presbyterian church, which looked ancient. People said it was built by British missionaries decades earlier, but who knows. It was made of well-worn red bricks and had a zinc roof. The walls were covered in flowery decorations, and a huge white cloth with a red embroidered cross covered an old wooden table, which served as the altar. The rafters, wrapped with glittering holiday ribbon, held it all firmly in place. It smelled inside like a mixture of custard apple, guava, and mango trees in the rain.

While the adults stayed cool and refreshed inside, kneeling and praying at the altar, the children gathered outside to "act wild," as though the devil himself had possessed us.

Name a game and we played it. Back-and-forth races,

skipping rope, climbing trees; we didn't have fancy sneakers or regulation balls and bats, as though that somehow made your God-given skills and athletic abilities more legitimate. Anything you could do with a little, we made a lot out of. And it didn't feel like missing out.

I was especially good at climbing between two trees, ping-ponging from left to right, with a trail of tinier children following after me like ducklings. Normally, I would have played like that for hours, but this time I got distracted. I jumped to the ground, leaned against one of the trees, and marveled at Oder, who was wiping the floor with everyone in every way.

No one could catch him, no one could outjump him, no one could outsmart him. No one impressed me more. And that's when it got funny, because everyone started ganging up on him. Two against one. Holding his leg. Jumping on his back as he raced throughout the compound. Grabbing his left arm as he attempted to chuck stones the farthest—he was a lefty, like me, which I was so proud of. Made me think I was like him and could be like him when I got older. Nothing could have made me happier than to follow in his footsteps and do everything he could as well as he could—hopefully, by his side.

Yet nothing could stop him. He was a force, but one with a positive spirit. One larger child got upset that Oder kept winning, and he refused to play anymore, sulking behind a tall, gangly tree. Oder patted him on the back and consoled him—he told him it just takes practice, like everything, and that he could get better and maybe one day surpass Oder in kids' games. That made the child feel better. It built up his confidence, and he challenged Oder to another race. We all gathered round to cheer the boy on. At which point Oder beat him soundly once more.

In the evening, after night prayers at the church, I had a moment to enjoy Oder's company on our walk home.

ME: I saw how fast you ran this evening. You were so fast, none of the kids could catch up.

ODER: I didn't run as fast as I wanted to. No one can run faster than me if I wear my favorite shorts.

I laughed. For Oder, taking a compliment was like showing weakness. He responded by showing more strength.

ME: One day I want to run as fast as you. Will you give me your shorts when they get old?

ODER: You already have a better pair of shorts than mine. You can use those to run and still be fast.

ME: Can we race home and see who wins? Let's see if I can run faster than you.

It was fun, teasing Oder. He didn't like to be teased, but he hated losing even more. Even though he didn't seem interested, I kept pushing.

ME : You have to give me a head start, because you have stronger feet than I.

What a weird thing to say, I know. Finally, he gave in.

ODER : Okay. You start running, then I will catch up with you.

I started running and, after covering some ground, turned to see if Oder was behind me. But he wasn't. He was gone. I hurried back in his direction to see if something had happened, or if he'd left me alone to get home in the dark by myself—which would have been uncharacteristically mean, but I figured it'd serve me right for pushing his buttons. I had run about twenty yards back, when all of a sudden Oder jumped from behind a tree trunk, where he'd been hiding, his hands formed into claws, as if he were a beast ready to devour me. He knew he didn't want to race, so he'd changed the game, and I fell right in line. I screamed with excitement.

Oder seemed to want to cultivate some form of independence in me, as if preparing me for a time when he wouldn't be around for me to imitate him or for him to protect me. Just like him, I was becoming good with my left hand, so I threw some punches at him, as though beating a monster back. Oder frowned. My attempt to be as cool as him was landing as softly as my jabs.

ODER : Ger, why are you so quick to toss punches around? You're going to hurt yourself or hurt someone else one of these days. And when that happens, no one will be there to defend you.

This left me feeling a bit ashamed and speechless. All I wanted was to be like him, do like him, impress and flatter him. But what he wanted—what he always seemed to be telling me—was for me to do my own thing. Be only me. Not follow him around or put so much stock in his validation. Yet his telling me not to care so much made me unsure if I should take this advice too. Big brothers can be so confusing, but you don't stop loving them, nevertheless.

ME: I'm sorry, big brother. I'll do better next time.

Oder smiled and nodded. But his gaze seemed distant. Like he wasn't sure when that next time would be. Or if there'd even be one. That brought me back down to earth, and we walked the rest of the way home in cricket silence.

JUSTICE

MY MUM, STEPMOTHER, COUSINS, AND siblings all gathered under one roof now to listen to Oder narrate his adventures. There's nothing like hearing it straight from the horse's mouth.

ODER: I was in the first group the SPLA took to Cuba. We traveled by boat from Ethiopia and were twenty-nine days in the water before we made one stop in Jamaica, where our boat was detained by Jamaica's government. They suspected Africans had been taken as slaves. We were allowed to continue on to Havana. So many young men and women vomited heavily on our journey. But you know me, I would not let something like seawater defeat me.

That had been in 1985. He explained how in Cuba, no one person could fight him. He was short, stocky, and well built, like my father, and was always on the front line, looking out for everyone else. SPLA chief of staff William Nyuon Bany Machar had called Oder into his office and expelled him because of his relationship with Bany's daughter. He thought Oder was distracting her from her studies and that he might get her pregnant. It's just as well because Oder was tired of dodging the liberation movement in Havana, and getting out was a blessing in disguise, even if it was for reasons our mother might not like to hear!

The fighting spirit had stayed inside Oder. And as much as I couldn't bear to admit it, I felt he would leave us at any time to go back to the front line. The war was not subsiding, and Oder was, first and foremost, an SPLA first lieutenant.

My cousin Gasim Gam walked with a little limp. Oder and Gasim would always spend time together, mostly talking late into the night.

One evening during dinner, Oder regaled us with the story of his shoulder injury, and the conversation between him and Gasim right after it happened.

GASIM: *Oder, my brother, sometimes I don't feel I am man enough because God reduced me to the one-legged man among his ten siblings. It's holding me back. I cannot even fight on the front lines with you.*

ODER: *Who we are is not the sum of our parts. All we need is educational opportunities, not strong legs to run on along the dangerous Sudan terrain. I was shot in the collarbone in Jokau Town's battle, but I did not escape simply because of my physicality.*

GASIM: *And what about me?*

ODER: *God has made it so that each of us will have our day in the sun. We all have our own strengths and will have our own vocations. You might be a lecturer in higher education, and a role model for young Ger.*

GASIM: *Your strength doesn't come from your muscles, does it? It comes from your mind.*

Sometime after Oder's return, as was routine, a large number of people were bathing at the Baro River. Without warning or reason, a seemingly frustrated soldier opened fire and started shooting indiscriminately. Before anyone could blink, hundreds of guns went off from all directions of the camp. In the ensuing melee, I was hit over the head with a brick. I passed out, and when I regained consciousness, the first sight I came across was that of my six-to-seven-months-pregnant stepmother, Nyagieng Chich, who was badly injured, together with my young cousin Gatriay Juch, who had suffered a bullet wound. He died due to lack of emergency medical attention.

We mourned for a long time. Meanwhile, some semblance of traditional justice was meted out—their killer was executed by a firing squad. At that point, I realized that Itang was no island of peace, for, like everywhere else we had been, human life remained cheap, taken away by a random bullet.

I formed my own little group, a pack of cousins, and began getting into up to seven fights a day. I was trying to follow in the footsteps of my brother Oder. But soon everyone was telling him that I was becoming a rough kid, fighting people older than myself.

One of my classmates and good friends, Gol Tut Khor, stuck to me like glue because he never wanted to fight, and I didn't mind boxing anyone who presented a problem. He was fond of what little arithmetic we learned and was the diplomat of the group. His reluctance to fight sometimes made me back down from unnecessary bouts—but maybe not often enough, because when word got back to Oder that I was causing trouble, he let me hear about it, in no uncertain terms.

Things got even worse when I started in with the gun talk.

ME: You know, I want a gun of my own.

ODER: You don't need a gun, Ger.

ME: I do! I need to protect myself and our family. You have a gun somewhere; you've used it too. And everyone respects you.

That did it. Oder got so worked up, I could swear he was at the point of physically harming me. He pinned me to the side of a building.

ODER: I didn't want this life. It was chosen for me. Stop being dumb, Ger. More proof that you need to go to school, not the army.

That stung.

ODER: Ger, you can end up a soldier like me, if you want to. You can become a farmer too, or a businessman like Dad. You can really be anything you want. All you need is an education.

The implication, which Oder didn't dare speak about aloud, was that the life of a soldier was a worst-case scenario. Our father believed in the SPLA cause so strongly that to suggest one of his sons not grow up to fight in the liberation war was to commit family treason. Oder, as the eldest son, who matured the very year the civil war began, had to fight. He had no choice, but I think Oder hoped that by the time I, who was eight years his junior, matured, I could forge my own path and be my own man. Not Dad. Not Tut. Not Oder. Just me.

ODER: There are reasons to fight, Ger. I'm not going to lie. Do you think our land has always had a dry season, and our people have always had to migrate to Upper Nile? No, it's because of the dams the Egyptians built on the Nile to steal our water. Arab treachery!

ME: I want to fight!

I screamed it, desiring only to grow up quickly and prove myself to him, to everyone.

ODER: You think you do, but why fight when you can't win? The Arabs have all the oil—they even have *our* oil!—and American support. We have a worthy cause, brother, but we can't win.

ME: What do you mean, we can't win? Dad's a fighter. He's fighting for us all. He would never fight for a lost cause.

ODER: What if I punched you here? Then here?

He thwacked me in the ribs. He was playing, but it still left an impression. He quickly added a light jab to my nose.

ODER: Then here, and here, and here!

I giggled as he play-boxed me with blows from every direction.

ODER: Your hands aren't tied, but you can't win against me, Ger. You're too small, and I'm too big.

ME: I'll fight harder!

I can't believe how young I sounded, how young of mind I was.

ODER: Yes. That's what I'm going to try to do, little brother. That's what Dad and I must try to do.

Something was eating him up. I couldn't understand why he wouldn't want me to become a fighter. He would tell me how close Havana and Florida were—that Cuba was in Latin America and only ninety miles from the United States—drawing me in. But then he'd say I would only be able to go to those places if I went to school and got an education, not if I became a soldier like him.

Still, my rule was that no one touched my sisters, brothers, or cousins, because I was their protector. Every day after school, there would be kids fighting. I would make sure I didn't miss any fights, whether I was participating or on the sidelines cheerleading. I enjoyed these skirmishes and treated them like they were a game: if I just got curious about someone, I'd immediately want to fight them.

My trick was never to show weakness, even if someone beat me up. One of the kids I had beaten up held a grudge against me, and one day while I was minding my business on the playing field, he appeared from nowhere and punched me in the nose. I fell down and almost passed out. But not too long after, I got up.

ME: Who punched me? Show your face!

No one wanted to reveal who he was. So in not wanting to show weakness, I burst out laughing hysterically, despite the pain and bloodied nose.

ME: Didn't hurt. Now, who wants to feel *real* pain?!

I wouldn't cry, no matter what, and this terrified everyone around me. After that, people either were my friend or just left me alone. It was an open secret on the playground that crossing my path wouldn't be pleasant. I had become a product of my environment and circumstances, taking in the effects of war and building a defense mechanism for myself and my family. And I was not going to let a little thing like the crippling fear I felt defeat me.

REALITY

I GOT TO ENJOY THE company of my brother for almost a year and a half. Then, in the middle of the night, Oder came and woke me.

> *ODER*: Wake up, Ger. Tonight you are once more the eldest son of all the family in Itang.

The moment I opened my eyes and saw the somber look on his face, I knew he was leaving. He sat me up and looked me straight in the eye.

> *ODER*: Ger, I want you to know that I will either kill or get killed in the Nasir fronts. But trust me on this: Don't grow up to be a soldier like me. Get an education. Make something of yourself.

Without any other word, Oder then slipped off into the darkness, leaving me alone, half-awake and half-asleep, to repeat his heavy words over and over in my mind. I was unsure if I would ever see him again or if I would be able to heed his advice, given that in the deep of night it felt like a dream. But the weight of Oder's words as he passed me the torch left me awakened to a new, more terrifying reality.

FATHER FIGURE

THE ARRIVAL OF EACH YEAR'S dry season demanded all able-bodied villagers herd cattle about a hundred and fifty miles to the Upper Nile Valley, where the animals could graze green, fertile grasslands. My older brother Duany, my younger sister Nyakuar, and I would urge the cattle along with gentle taps of a stick, while Mum carried the twins in the *dieny* balanced on her head.

We became a caravan of herders as we picked up people along the way, a train thousands of bodies strong. Usually we would come across friendly faces—people who would take you in if you were in trouble, almost like extended family, even if you were a stranger. But there were plenty of times we would encounter town busybodies . . . or worse. That was even the case when we walked through our own village of Liet.

MUM: Look away, Ger. These people have the evil eye.

My mother would take the extraordinary step of covering up my baby sister, Nyandit, to shield her from their gaze.

MUM: We must keep her safe. She is more vulnerable and susceptible to those who would do her harm. Protect her at all costs.

ME: Okay, Mum. I promise I will.

I wasn't exactly sure what evil Mum saw in these people, except for maybe jealousy or envy. But as we journeyed toward the Greater Upper Nile region, most of that pettiness fell away, since we were all in the same boat—traveling together for the same purpose: survival.

There, we united with other neighboring villages in a kind of huge summer camp, where we danced, sang, gossiped, played, and celebrated the bounty of the Nile well into the starlit evenings. This journey, which we Nuer people call "way of way," defined the rhythm of our lives, with our summer camps having been there for centuries, giving us the opportunity to meet up once a year with our ethnic families, whom everyone knew by sight and through story. On top of that, the group of thousands became an extended family. Every child was your brother or sister, and every adult your parent, or at least your auntie or uncle. It made making mischief a lot more difficult and, in turn, a lot more fun.

But once the wet season came in West Akobo, our family

would walk home again. And this particular year was the hardest of all. Not because the trek was made any more difficult by the heavy rain that overflowed the Nile River, but because of the other thing that awaited us once we got back. . . .

Good-byes now came regularly. Oder, gone. Then Chuol. And next came my twelve-year-old brother, Duany. Although he headed for a different SPLA base—in Dima, Ethiopia, where they were trained as child soldiers from the battalion of Zalzal—the end result was the same: more loss and heartache.

His departure immediately elevated me to the eldest boy of the family, a responsibility I took seriously. Now eight, I was charged with safekeeping my younger siblings, the way Oder had taken care of me. I continued doing my best to babysit the twins and look after Nyakuar. I enjoyed the responsibility, but also, I just loved those babies.

The twins had been born between eleven and midnight during harvesttime, around October or November. The boy twin, Both—a traditional name for a male twin meaning "leading"—was loud and assertive, mischievous from day one. Mum always had to get up in the middle of the night to deal with his crying, but when she shushed him gently, he usually turned docile as a lamb. Each evening, Mum would sing this song softly to her little trouble-maker:

A joyful little boy who was never a sinner was forgiven.

Are there any boys who were to come to God?
So let's all go to God to wash our sins together.
A joyful little girl who was never a sinner was forgiven too.
Are there any girls who were told not to come to God?
Let's all go together, let's all hold hands together.
O Jehovah, hear my prayers.
Even though I am constantly breaking your commandments,
Even when I miss your path,
You still continue to forgive and guide me.
And when judgment day comes, take my soul to heaven,
And let my body return to earth.

I'd close my eyes and listen to her soothing voice; it was as though her lilting words wrapped around me like a blanket and lulled me to sleep as well.

The girl twin, Nyandit, which means "second person," was the opposite of Both. I spent long minutes looking into her bright brown eyes and admiring her wide forehead. She was silent and keen and stared back at me, like she could not only read all the thoughts in my head but also understand them. Like she knew where my life was headed and wanted to tell me all about it, but the pesky reality of her being a baby prevented her from divulging it.

Her hair grew in yellow, like mine, and I loved that we had this in common.

MUM: Ger, you and Nyandit have the same straight teeth, but she has a perfect gap. Too bad for you after your baby teeth fell out, Ger.

I think Nyandit held as special a place in my mother's heart as she did in mine. She was so sweet and cute, Mum used to take extra precautions to protect her, such as covering her when someone looked at her wrong.

At times, I was charged with taking the twins to the Pibor River to bathe. I could barely restrain Both from jumping from my arms and plopping into the water. A dip in the river was a treat, and he loved the feel of the current brushing against his skin like satin, engulfing his whole body.

For Nyandit, it was the opposite. I tried to lower her down into the waves, and I quickly realized that was not going to happen. Her body shook and quaked and shivered as though she'd been bitten by a snake, and she clung to me like a cat would if you even thought about putting it in the same room as a tub. When I grabbed her teensy wrist to try to release her unimaginably tight grip, I felt through her pulsating veins her heart pounding, as resonant as a kettledrum.

ME: Nyandit, let go, please. It will be okay. Look at Both! He is enjoying the water.

But she wouldn't budge.

ME: Water is our friend. Nothing exists without it. Water means life. Plus, you must bathe. You stink.

I resigned myself to sinking lower into the river so Nyandit, who was almost strangling me with her arms double-wrapped around my neck, could glance her foot off the surface and I could tell Mum she at least touched the water this time.

When Both was fully clean, I brought the twins to the riverbank, removed my maroon shirt, dipped it in the river, and washed Nyandit that way. We had that battle every time the twins were due for a bath. Eventually, it became more of an amusement for me, but it never got funnier to Nyandit. Other than this one irrational quirk, she was the most docile, agreeable being you could ever meet.

According to my culture, twins are special. They are classified as part human, part bird, because just as a bird lays two or more eggs at one time, twins are a double blessing. Additionally, we liken twins to angels because they are innocent, harmless souls, fragile and vulnerable, requiring extra respect and care. They are also seen as messengers from ancestors passed on who bring news, such as of rain, tragedy, drought, famine, or, in Both and Nyandit's case, a great harvest.

It is thought that the second person out was created first in the mother's womb but didn't want to go first. I could see this being the case with Nyandit. She was not the adventurous one; she was more interested in Both testing the waters, so to speak, before she'd take her own little baby leap of faith. And that was fine with me. If ever an eight-year-old could feel like a father, I did. Nyandit was that special to me.

HYENAS

I FELT EMPTY AND DEJECTED after Oder left for the front line, but Itang provided some stability. We'd been moving around like nomads, and Itang gave me a sense of belonging to a physical place, somewhere I could consider home, even if just for a while. I played soccer with my age-mates and went to the beach in the afternoons and evenings, performed mock military parades and learned the alphabet. This gave me a sense of progress, like I was getting somewhere in life. The SPLA, on the other hand, gave me a sense of hope for the future, since there was talk that once we were older, we would be taken to school in Kenya, something that I looked forward to. And by now we had built homes and were no longer living in huts. It was the first feeling of permanence that I'd had in a long time.

On occasion, I would practice my karate in camp, which was another way to keep Oder's spirit with me, even if I wasn't allowed to discuss how he was. There was a man named Gatdor who saw me training by the bank of the river and struck up a conversation with me.

GATDOR: Where did you learn to do these stunts?

ME: My older brother showed me. I've been training ever since.

GATDOR: Do you think you could outmaneuver a machine gun with your fancy footwork?

ME: Not the machine gun, but maybe the man firing it.

Gatdor laughed. He thought me a bit cheeky but didn't take offense. After that, he was friendly and would ask me what I had done to be better in the long run.

ME: I am loaded and ready to deliver.

Gatdor slowly walked toward me, then ordered me to do a standing front tuck. Which I did—quite well, I might add.

It was around this time that my father started sneaking in and visiting us for short spells when he wasn't fighting for the SPLA. Dad's spies seemed to suggest Anya Anya II spies were few and far between in camp, so it was somewhat safer for him to be around. With Dad in the house, it felt like one hero had gone but a new one had returned to take his place. If only all our family could be together again under one roof. If I'd had a thousand birthdays, it would have been my one and only wish.

A strange occurrence became commonplace in the camp: every evening there would be wailing from one home or another, news having gotten back from the front line that a family member—a son, father, or uncle—had died from enemy fire.

My schoolmate Moses's father, Captain Bikhan Deng, was a senior SPLA soldier. One day Moses told me that his dad was back from fighting on the front line, and I accompanied Moses home after school. I couldn't think about decorum or manners and blurted out my questions.

ME: How was the fighting? Is Oder okay? My brother?

CAPTAIN DENG: It is nice to meet you, young man. And everything is great at the front line. We fight like the fate of the world rests on our shoulders. Your brother too. You should be proud.

However, the following day, Captain Deng came over to my family's home. He found my father and mother and me and asked us to move closer. I instantly felt something was wrong. He offered no formalities.

CAPTAIN DENG: I am sorry to be the one to have to tell you this, but your son, your brother Oder has been shot dead by soldiers from the north.

When we heard this coldly delivered news, voices from inside our home rose up in that familiar melancholic chorus that had quickly supplanted the chirping of insects as the soundtrack of the evening. Noises escaped my mum's and my lips that none of us had ever before emitted, coming from wells inside that none of us had ever before tapped. They reminded me of the vivid screams I'd heard as a small boy that are implanted in my brain of a lion behind our hut defending itself against an attack by ten to fifteen hyenas. My father, shocked, sat still, neither moving nor blinking. We had cried tears of joy in that same spot when Oder had come back. Now we were crying because Oder was dead, killed in the battle of Nasir.

DAD: Everyone, stop crying now. You are giving me a headache.

Father exited the house after Captain Deng, leaving my mother and me to grieve with each other.

I was inconsolable and couldn't sleep that night. I looked outside and saw my father seated alone in the dark. He was hunched over, his big frame looking almost like a pile of sticks in the moonlight, his shoulders heaving. He was crying softly. This began the first and only period of time I ever saw him cry. I quietly observed him cry at night for several nights. Oder's death was easily one of the biggest blows to my family, since everyone was fond of him. And the way it went down. From Captain Deng telling me everything was okay, then coming the following day to tell my family of Oder's death, to my father's show of strength in public and weeping in private, it became clear to me that the SPLA wanted to keep deaths hidden. For acknowledging them in the open would yield a drastic drop in anyone's enthusiasm for this—or any—war.

PART II

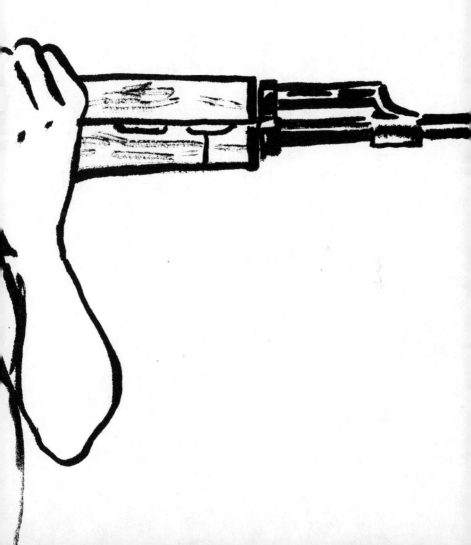

THE BULLET THIEF

RUMORS ABOUNDED WITHIN THE SPLA that we needed to go back to Sudan—the situation in Ethiopia was becoming untenable. We chalked it up to hyperbole and rumor. Then in 1991, when I was about thirteen years old, an Ethiopian jet fighter opened fire on Itang, forcing hundreds of thousands of us to flee for our lives. Ethiopia's Mengistu Haile Mariam had been deposed by rebel forces who, in league with our enemy, northern Sudan, wanted all southern Sudanese refugees out of Ethiopian territory.

We were now sandwiched between two wars—the first one among the Ethiopians, who now sought to eject us from their country, and the second one between the SPLA and the government in Khartoum.

I was around the UN food-rationing area when the attacks started. It was the rainy season and the Nile was overflowing. I ran to my stepmother Elizabeth's house. She had already fled. I ran to my mother's house. She too had fled. My family had fled toward the forest. I was alone, stranded.

Everyone with strength ran toward one of two places, the UN storage facility or the SPLA armory within the camp. The UN facility had food supplies, while the SPLA armory had guns and bullets. I ran toward the armory, where I witnessed indiscriminate killing as people fought over guns. One person would go into the armory and come out with four guns. Someone else, wielding a gun, would see them.

GUN WIELDER: You have four guns. Give me two!

LOOTER: Get out of my way. I got here first!

And now a gunfight would ensue. It was unbelievable to see those under siege fight among themselves. This just went to show how valuable guns were to my people at the time.

Seeing this, I decided I wouldn't take a gun from the armory, because if someone saw a kid with a gun, they would certainly have taken it away from me. Instead, I decided to grab a bag of bullets, which I intended to trade for food along the way. I knew there would be an excess of guns but a shortage of bullets. Luck was on my side because the bag of bullets I picked was for the M16, rare and expensive. AK-47 bullets were affordable and more readily available.

I came across a stray donkey wandering around, its

owner having fled. This was a relief because I couldn't have managed to carry the heavy bag of bullets a long distance. I put the bag on the donkey and started walking toward the health facility. When I got there, I found a group of gunmen ransacking the place, throwing patients off beds and stealing the mattresses. The storage room for medicine was also ransacked and mostly emptied. Given all this destruction and chaos, I realized we might never return to Itang.

What surprised me was that amid the violence and chaos of that moment, I thought of nothing else but school. I was heartbroken, knowing that the only chance I had gotten of receiving an education was now being blown by the fighting. As I walked through the melee at the hospital, looking like an innocent bystander, I picked up an old, muddied magazine from the floor. I perused it and was visually struck by what I later learned was a map of Africa. I ripped out that particular page and put it in my pocket and proceeded to take my own little share of the medicine from the floor of the plundered storage room.

When I emerged back into the fray, I found my stray donkey, with my bullets still on it, and got moving toward Sudan. I didn't necessarily know the direction; all I had to do was follow the mass of people. As we moved, there were incidents of people violently snatching things from each other. The operating rule seemed to be that any possession was a valuable possession in wartime. This made me disguise myself further as a harmless child, not wanting to attract attention and have my bullets and medicine taken away. Walking the donkey—which was unwise, given that we were all trying to get away as fast as possible—provided me with further cover, making me appear confused.

I kept looking for my brothers and pregnant mother as I walked along. When night came, no one seemed to be sleeping. There was gunfire all around. Guns being a hot commodity, everyone with a firearm was a target. If you had a gun, someone else wanted it. People even preyed upon SPLA soldiers because they were no longer the only ones who were armed. Others were shooting at imaginary enemies. I got tired and passed out in the middle of nowhere. The elderly and sick had been left behind in Itang. This was the most chaotic war I had ever seen.

I was completely terrified, thinking of the journey ahead of me to get back to war-torn Sudan. And during the night, I thought the most about my pregnant mother. It was wet and cold, and I couldn't imagine her facing such harsh weather in her condition. I thought I had become a man, an adult, worrying about others, though I was hardly in my teens. I was hoping that my mother had somehow reconnected with Chuol and Duany, who before this attack had returned to Itang from their SPLA training. In that case, she would be fine, since my older brothers could fend for her and protect her no matter how difficult things got. And, boy, had Oder been alive . . .

Throughout the days, I kept the image of my mother in my mind's eye and she kept me company, her high cheekbones rising even higher as she smiled at me. Under my breath I repeated the stories she used to tell me—about how the zebra got its stripes or the dog lost its voice. I missed her ability to make sense of everything.

The group of people I was moving with finally settled at a place called Makoat. It was a raised dry area, surrounded by a swampy area, on the bank of the Nile. I thought I would find my mother there, since a group had already arrived. With a friendly Nuer family, I traded some of my bullets and pills for food, which kept me alive for a few days. After spending a week in Makoat wandering around like a madman looking for my family, I bumped into my auntie Nyantek, her son Wunbil Koak Duany, and her partner, Mr. Guok Ruach. They had just arrived from a nearby locale called Kiirinbor. Auntie used to make fun of Guok, insisting he was her "partner in crime," because in Nuer culture there's no such thing as a widow having a "boyfriend."

They told me my mother and brothers had taken refuge at Kiirinbor, and were frantic, not knowing my whereabouts, desperately looking for me.

UNCLE GUOK: You, Wunbil, will take Ger to rejoin his family in Kiirinbor.

WUNBIL: Fine. But he will have to leave that stupid donkey or it will slow us down.

As much as I hated to, I left my donkey, bullets, and medicine in Makoat, and the two of us made our way to Kiirinbor.

When we arrived, we found my mother lying under a

tree, where she had recently given birth to Gok, who was wrapped in the few items of clothing she had brought along. My mother, a bit frail, pulled me close to touch my head, as if that was the spot to check on my health. Then she held me in a tight embrace.

MUM: You had us worried, Ger. But I am happy you made it. Meet your little brother.

Gok, who would grow up to have most of my features, just lay there, comfortable in the little castle my mother had built him of twigs stuck in the ground and draped with blankets to protect him from the sun and wind. I looked at his tender hands, wanting to play with him. Here was one more person I was now responsible for, since I could no longer pass for a child.

MUM: Ger, get yourself some rest. You must be tired.

GUNS AND THIEVES

WITH MY MOTHER WERE MY little sister Nyakuar, the twins Both and Nyandit, and my older brothers Chuol and Duany, who, along with some of their SPLA friends like Stephen Malual, had a mini army of guns among them to keep the family secure. My uncles, aunties, and cousins were all under their guard. Chuol had been trained as a tank driver and had three guns: an AK-47 and an M16, plus a PT92 pistol that he kept strapped around his waist at all times.

I was overjoyed to be reunited with the twins, Nyandit especially. We all packed our few belongings the following day to head back to Makoat. I asked if I could be the one to carry the twins on our journey.

Unfortunately, once we arrived, we found out there was no food there. Due to the relentless hunger, two of my friends, Thon and Gony, decided to get creative one night.

We had been starving the whole day, and Gony, who was older than Thon and me, had spotted a family with goats and came up with the idea of stealing one. At first I didn't agree, but they weren't relenting. We didn't mention this to Chuol or Duany. So, at nightfall, Gony and Thon crept out of the sleeping area and pulled me outside to embark on our mission, carrying a blunt knife with us.

We got to the area where the goats were sleeping and chose the one we wanted to slaughter. The moment we nabbed it, the rest scattered in different directions, screaming for their lives. I grabbed the goat's back legs as Gony and Thon grabbed its front. Gony, the strongest among us, grabbed its mouth and nose and started cutting its throat with the blunt knife. The goat was kicking and shoving, trying to make all kinds of noise, and in no time its owner was wide-awake. And wielding a gun.

He burst out into the open, and the moment I saw him, I let go of the goat and sprinted into the night, leaving Thon and Gony behind. I hid in the bushes just far enough away to be able to witness what was about to happen, in case the man harmed Thon and Gony. I heard him shouting in Nuer.

GOAT OWNER: If you try to run, I will shoot. You have killed my goat. I will kill you today.

Thon and Gony were frozen with fear.

GOAT OWNER: Where are you from?

THON: We are Nuer. We just came from Itang. We are here with our families.

GOAT OWNER: Where are your families? Where are your possessions? How many were you?

THON: We were three.

When I heard this, I started running.

I got back to where my family was and sneaked into my sleeping place. Within no time, Thon, Gony, and the goat's owner arrived. Thon and Gony came to wake me up, and I pretended I was dead asleep. My brothers Chuol and Duany and their SPLA friends heard the commotion and reached for their guns.

DUANY: What is going on here?!

By this time, the goat's owner, who had brought the half-slaughtered goat with him, was pointing his gun at us.

GOAT OWNER: I will shoot everyone here!

Stephen started shouting, pointing his gun at the goat's owner.

STEPHEN: This is nonsense. No one can come here and threaten us. If this is the day we die, then let us all die.

This was going to get ugly.

GOAT OWNER: These kids were stealing my goat. They have slaughtered it.

CHVOL: Ger, did you do it? Tell us now. Did you steal the goat?

Before I could reply, the rest of the group was joining Stephen, guns trained at the goat's owner. I didn't wait to see what would happen next.

ME: Everyone, please wait a minute. Yes, we slaughtered the man's goat.

I was trying to save the situation. I told my brothers to hold their horses. I would take responsibility.

CHVOL: What do you mean, you will take responsibility?

ME: I will pay the man.

Everyone thought I was crazy, saying I would settle the matter with the goat's owner, knowing I didn't have the means to do so. But they were mistaken. I had the bag of bullets hidden away.

CHVOL: How much do you want from us?

GOAT OWNER: I want another goat. The size of the one they have slaughtered.

ME: I can give you a hundred bullets.

This caught everyone by surprise. We lit a huge bonfire so we could see outside, and I sneaked away to get the bag of bullets from my hiding place. I spread my blanket on the ground and started counting the bullets. No one wanted to eat the goat anymore, so the man took the bullets and the goat.

My actions had just exposed the fact that my family had a lot of guns, so we resolved to leave Makoat. It was no longer safe. An attack on the family, whether by the goat owner or anyone else, was imminent.

CLEAN CONSCIENCE

NOW, IN 1991, THERE WERE two dominant SPLA factions, each led by a strongman representing one of the two largest ethnic groups in southern Sudan. Dr. John Garang, a Dinka, ran one faction, while Dr. Riek Machar, a Nuer, headed the splinter group. They had many differences—including personal ambition and temperament—but their ideological divide was what eventually broke the camel's back. Dr. Garang and his brigade believed in the idea of a New Sudan, where Muslims and Christians would live side by side in peaceful coexistence. Dr. Machar, taking the Anya Anya II separatist route, championed a split of the predominantly Christian south from the predominantly Arab north. Funnily enough, their visions were more or less the same: more independence for the south, and an end of domination by the north.

This fluid landscape of the civil war meant that not only were the northern Sudanese, based in Khartoum, bombing our region in the south, but the SPLA's two factions were now going at each other. Anyone who resisted the will of either faction became an automatic target. Every southern Sudanese was now at war: each against the other, and all of them against Khartoum.

We had a family meeting before leaving Makoat because, on top of war everywhere, there was also a dangerous flood!

MUM: To ensure all of us have enough food to survive on, we will split up. I and the smallest children, including Ger and Duany, will head toward Nasir. I am told there is relief food there from humanitarian agencies.

CHUOL: And I and the rest of us will head to Diik to join my father and Nyaluak Guech.

Our family would never be whole again.

Nasir wasn't the haven we had hoped it would be. A huge population had moved back from Itang, and there was no way of sustaining the numbers. Because of the food shortage in Nasir, Duany and I decided to leave our mother with our little siblings and head to a village called Diik within West Akobo (otherwise known as Waat Town) to join our father. Once there, I shared the scant food available with him and Nyaluak, while Duany stayed with Uncle Reat's family. Uncle Reat never left Diik Village in Waat Town Sudan, no matter how bad the fighting got. He always stayed behind, working the land and taking care of the one place we would all come back to from wherever we would wander across the world. He remained an enduring feature of the place we called home.

A group of men from around our home had been part of Dr. Machar's SPLA faction, and they had just returned from a raid in the Bor area, where a lot of killing, looting, and destruction of property had taken place. One of my father's friends had brought back a huge herd of cattle, and for a time, it seemed like there was enough meat to go around the entire village. The men back from the front line brought tales of the differences between Dr. Machar and Dr. Garang, and my father, who had fought alongside Dr. Garang for many years, now seemed to be siding with his tribesman, Dr. Machar! The ethnic divide was growing wider within the SPLA.

My father was happy I had made it to his home and that my mother and the rest of the family were safe back in Nasir. I spent my days tending his cattle and continued to feel that he was trusting me more, sensing that I had grown into a responsible young man. He allowed me to clean his guns, having noticed my skill when he watched me dismantle some and put them back together.

DAD: Hey, Ger, make sure you clean the guns today.

It became a regular instruction from my father, since we had a little armory inside our home. Whenever my father came back from a successful military operation, he would always allow me to take his gun and shoot in the air in celebration. These were the signs, to me, that he trusted me. Yet another reason why I decided not to rock the boat and ask about his shift in allegiance.

With the division in the SPLA, people's personal security became their own responsibility, and families had to arm themselves. The attack in Bor resulted in deep-rooted animosity between the Dinka and the Nuer. Instead of seeing it as one SPLA faction attacking another, they viewed it purely through an ethnic prism. It was in this context of everyone looking out for themselves that my father honored me by giving me an AK-47 of my own.

> **DAD**: Ger, use this to keep cattle rustlers at bay and defend the family against attacks from rival ethnic groups.

I expected we would have a further conversation about the gun, but that never happened. In a sense, my father assumed I already knew my responsibilities, the dos and don'ts of owning a gun. Being a man of few words, he believed I was grown enough to have seen my people's way of life, and to know that a gun was not a toy but rather an instrument of both safety and death.

I quickly became known for firing the weapon fiercely in the direction of any danger I sensed, whether real or imaginary, possibly out of the excitement of finally having my father's full confidence and feeling equal to SPLA fighters. I became a sharpshooter, rarely missing my target. I also started shooting for sport, and whenever aimless shooting was heard around my village, once he got home, my father would ask whether that had been me shooting for pleasure. It was something he seemed not to mind, since shooting for sport was my way of showing I had a good relationship with my AK-47.

One night not long after, cattle raiders attacked our village. To prove to my father that he had not made a wrong decision, I made sure I was among the fastest-running warriors going after the cattle. We ran with our guns heavy on our shoulders and I got tired along the way, but I couldn't show any weakness—not even that I was afraid I might shoot someone dead. As we ran ahead, my father and the other older men stayed farther behind, watching us. I earned my place, and my father witnessed my capabilities. We recovered the cattle, chasing the attackers deep into the forest, where they disappeared.

I knew the implications of owning a gun—that in a split second I could take away a life, just as mine too could be taken, but my overarching philosophy was that all I was doing was protecting my family, being a proper Nuer man.

Although I was no stranger to guns, this was the first one I had ever owned. As I cleaned it most evenings, I wondered whether it would lead to my downfall or be my lifeline. It was at such times that the words of my late warrior brother, Oder, echoed in my mind: *Trust me on this: Don't become a soldier like me. Get an education.* In my defense, I told myself that I had gone to Itang to seek an education, but then the Ethiopians had sent us back to Sudan, and now I didn't know what the future portended. In the meantime, my gun was all I had. That night, I wiped it clean.

A SOLDIER IS BORN

CHILD SOLDIERS BROUGHT INTO THE army wouldn't really have a first day on the job, since by the time they started, they would already know how to march in a military parade, handle guns, keep secrets, and sing SPLA war songs. They would be deployed to fetch firewood and make meals, getting instructed not to venture too far out of camp. Boys who were joining the army ranks had already been indoctrinated to believe nothing but the SPLA's narrative.

I began my time in the SPLA stationed in Baliet, within two subsections of Dinka Ngok and Eastern Nuer territory led by Dr. Machar. I initially was a gun cleaner, doing now for the military what I'd once done for my father as a domestic chore.

My specific posting was as part bodyguard and part assistant to SPLA First Lieutenant Peter Gatdor, the man from Itang who had developed a fondness for me through my karate training. Other than taking care of the wounded,

I would do personal chores for him and his associates, like rolling their tobacco and running small errands that were not necessarily military-related.

It wasn't glamorous work, but it kept me close enough to the senior officers such that they too grew to like me and grant me special favors, like the ability to access portions of military food and pass it on to my starving family. Normally, food supplies were taken to a central storage facility. From there they would get distributed to different SPLA camps. But I'd found a way to use my position and friendships to my and my family's benefit. I neither regretted nor felt any shame for this.

Each week, when food was transported to the Nasir side and delivered to the satellite military camps, I managed to get on the truck by buttering up the senior SPLA guys.

ME: Bol Mel, Tank 55! How are things on the front lines?

BOL MEL: We are holding up strong. But I suggest you leave Baliet for Nasir Town, young Ger!

ME: I am better off in Baliet because famine will finish me in Nasir Town.

BOL MEL: Know where your brother Chuol is? He's in Ketbek Town with Dr. Riek Machar.

ME: Bol Mel, I hate to ask, but my mother and my sisters and brothers are starving in Nasir Town, I swear to God. I want to visit them sometime, but I can't go empty-handed.

BOL MEL: Okay, I will speak with John Noor. He'll help you get there with a sack of maize, but make sure not to come back to Baliet.

ME: *Shukran,* my brother!

BOL MEL: Say hello to Chuol Thabach, my brother!

But I was not going to Ketbek. Having already secured a little maize for my mother before securing a spot on the truck, I'd sometimes sleep underneath it to ensure I'd be nearby when it was set to depart. I'd mark my bag using charcoal so that no one else picked it up once we got to Nasir, then I'd sneak over IED-strewn roads to get this food to my mother.

We didn't have adequate supplies due to the split in the SPLA. This meant the majority of soldiers didn't wear proper military gear. Some wore flip-flops, others worn-out, hand-me-down uniforms. We were starting to look more like a ragtag militia than an army, and the line between who was SPLA and who wasn't grew thinner by the day, since everyone around us owned a gun to protect himself. There was a growing need for soldiers, and the only qualifications were loyalty and the ability to operate a gun. While some Dinkas were loyal to Dr. Machar, and some Nuers to Dr. Garang, for the most part, their fellow soldiers did not trust them and saw them as spies for the other side.

• • •

It was in the early days of combat that I was unexpectedly reunited with Peter Gatkuoth, my old friend from Itang, who was now sixteen to my thirteen. We hugged like long-lost brothers, which we essentially were: the boys of Sudan. He still loved a good joke and entertained us with little stand-up comedy routines about our predicament.

PETER: *Once upon a time, a skeleton man bumped into a human cannibal in the forest. The human cannibal exclaimed, "Skeleton man!"*

"Yes, sir," the skeleton said.

"Where were you heading? And where were you coming from with such long, skinny legs?"

The skeleton man replied, "I went to visit a friend, but I am going to Bentui Town."

"Well, I want to eat you now, but you look so skinny, like you could poison me," said the human cannibal.

"I'd definitely poison you," said the skeleton man, "because I have no fat on my body."

Said the cannibal, "What if I kill you and mix your meat with a fat man's meat? Don't you think you'll taste better?"

"No, I won't taste like anything in your mouth. In fact, I will spoil your good stuff," the skeleton man replied.

The human cannibal shot back, "You are right. I've never seen a man as thin as you. Please get out of my sight before I change my mind."

The skeleton man bid the cannibal farewell: "Good-bye, and if you have any ideas, catch up with me."

"Before I let you go," the cannibal said, "here's what I think: What if I kill you today and dry your meat for next season? Do you think it will taste better?"

The skeleton man said, "You'll be wasting your time. My entire body is made of veins like a camel's."

And with that, the cannibal had had enough: "You're so honest with me. Please go to Bentui Town and keep your mouth shut!"

Together we formed a tight group, along with a small, fierce seventeen-year-old we called Airborne Boy, who was a celebrity in the army for his skilled storytelling and the bloody battles he'd survived, often using counterinsurgency strategies.

AIRBORNE BOY: My close friend Waad got caught up in a dreadful Antonov An-225 aircraft attack. I survived the bombardment because I stayed in my trench, but Waad got chopped up into little pieces.

I listened, rapt, just as I had when my mother told me tales under the cover of night when I was a little boy. Though she'd meant for the stories to put me to sleep, they instead excited me. Airborne Boy always had a cheekful of chewing tobacco and spat the brown juice out as punctuation. The three of us laughed together, slept side by side, and were nearly inseparable.

A SOLDIER IS DEAD

I WAS SCARED OF GOING to war, but I had been surrounded by death for so long now that it had an air of inevitability to it. The first time I saw combat was in 1992, when I was about fourteen. The platoon I was with—a mix of child soldiers, young cats, and older army men—attacked a group from Torit, one of the areas aligned with Dr. Garang. There was a military parade to select men after word came that the enemy was approaching. First Lieutenant Gatdor, to whom I was attached, gave me his military bag to carry. He told me we were going to war. Though the enemy had more guns and bullets, we had more manpower. We realized that if the enemy attacked first, there was a real possibility they would overrun us, hence our need to be proactive and go on the offense. I walked along with the fighters, approaching the front line.

We opened fire wildly, and miraculously gained ground, marching through a field of bodies. My hands shook and my heart pounded as we shouted our rallying cry.

SOLDIERS: *SPLA Oyee!*

At that moment, it all felt right, and with adrenaline spurring me on, I acted unfazed by the spilled blood of my fallen comrades. As much as it shocked me, I felt I was the warrior I was always meant to be. When we returned from the front line, I searched for First Lieutenant Gatdor's bag but couldn't find it. I went to bed, but soon he was shaking me awake.

FIRST LIEUTENANT GATDOR: Ger, where is my bag?

ME: I put it somewhere and didn't see it when I went to get it.

First Lieutenant Gatdor got wild and started screaming at me.

FIRST LIEUTENANT GATDOR: How could you lose my bag? How could you lose my bag?!

Before I knew it, he was smacking me. There was a lot of theft at the time, everyone just trying to survive, but I had been tasked with what seemed like something simple, and I had failed to keep his possession safe.

Even more than during times of peace, one's meager possessions take on added value during times of war. There was a European journalist and aid worker named

Simon wandering around the camp, and we were fascinated by him. He wore shorts and military boots, and we always hung around him to hear how he spoke English through the nose. Simon had a really huge camera with long lenses, which went missing one day. Simon suspected the thief was a soldier from the Nuba Mountains. The man was apprehended and beaten for days by senior soldiers before being locked up in a makeshift jail. It was highly unlikely that the man was the guilty party, but he was the enemy and therefore an easy person on whom to pin the blame. It was terrifying, watching what happened to him, and it did not seem as though the punishment fit the crime.

I flashed back to the time I had to watch my uncle Tut get humiliated and tortured by Anya Anya II soldiers. It was a year after his initiation. He had trained in Bonga with Oder in a separate battalion and then returned to our village for a short family visit. That's when Anya Anya II caught him. His reputation as a good soldier preceded him, and they wanted to both break and recruit him while frightening the rest of us villagers into submission. They accused him of stealing a gun, and they tied his hands and legs to his back. He was so compressed he reminded me of travel luggage. His chest was pressed into the hot sand as they beat him down like a donkey. I couldn't stop screaming.

ME: *LET GO OF MY UNCLE. HE DIDN'T STEAL YOUR GUN!*

Uncle Tut just moaned and rolled on the ground, without any tears streaming out of his eyes, until almost all life was drained from his body. Ultimately, they'd forced my uncle to join their ranks instead of the SPLA and fight for their cause. That itself was a different kind of torture—one of the soul. I felt the same pain now watching this soldier's brutal humiliation over the missing camera.

I climbed inside my mosquito net that evening and closed my eyes, hoping sleep might release me from the agony of wakefulness and the horrors of real life. I dreamed of my mother, of hugging her and being home again, safe. She squirmed a bit in my grasp, which I did not understand. Why would a mother deliberately shun her own child? As my eyelids creaked open, she slunk farther from me, then turned to face me dead-on. I recognized that look. I was staring into the gaze of a deadly python. I stifled a scream and threw the snake away from me as I leaped backward and fumbled for my gun. The python slithered out of the netting and away into the night. Sleep was no longer even a temporary comfort. No escape.

Later I was called away from Baliet for a few weeks to fight, and we stumbled upon a group of men lined up to be executed by firing squad. I did not allow myself to look away from these men who were facing their deaths head-on. Some were scared, others blank, as though their spirits had been drained from their bodies long ago and they were walking shells of who they once were, their humanity already dead.

But that was nothing compared to what followed. Soon

we faced an attack in Baliet by a vicious warlord named General George Athor, a Dinka Ngok, a subtribe of the Dinka already supporting the Garang arm of the SPLA. General Athor was known for his bravery and strategic military mind. He had been a soldier in Sudan's military before joining the SPLA. He was short, stout, and brainy, and word was that if he attacked, you wouldn't survive.

General Athor had disguised his troops as civilians and they infiltrated our camp, milling about, waiting for the perfect opportunity to strike. He and his gunmen surrounded the camp around four a.m., before the sun had come up, and one could hardly see. Guns were trained on us, including RPGs. Everything was happening so fast, and everyone would have to jump into the Nile to stand a chance of survival, First Lieutenant Gatdor included.

Our faction of the SPLA didn't have enough guns to go around, and so I found myself terrified and without a weapon as the enemies forced our troops—many of whom couldn't swim—toward the Nile. I had done this dance before, but this time I was not an innocent civilian, I was the enemy. Although I could swim, I knew I'd most likely get shot in the river, and so I jumped into the passenger seat of a military truck parked nearby. I didn't know how to drive. The bullets whizzed past, and I recognized it was only a matter of time before they found me and filled my body with holes.

Suddenly the vehicle's door swung open, and there was First Lieutenant Gatdor! I couldn't believe my luck. In a split second, he'd already jammed his foot on the gas and sped off from the fighting across the grasslands, bullets pinging off the truck as we fled.

Airborne Boy and his girlfriend, Nyankor, were in their little grass room, sleeping in the nude, when soldiers sneaked in and shot them dead. I had no clue what happened to Peter and could not stay to find out. It is hard to explain to people what it feels like to leave someone you care about behind with the knowledge that doing so most certainly means they will die. But my mother and I had done so before with my dad, and then my mother had done so with me, and now I was doing so with my best friend. It's the kind of thing you do everything in your power not to think about ever again. To swallow, bury inside your bones, and forget.

Countless others were shot in the Nile, and Baliet was completely flattened. About ninety people, soldiers and civilians, were killed on that one day. The bullets did not discriminate between them. I took the news hard and considered it payback or karma for the suffering of the soldier accused of stealing Simon's camera equipment.

The attackers took vehicles, guns, and prisoners. Most of those captured were from the Nuba Mountains and didn't know how to swim. Bodies floated on the Nile, and word got around that people in Malakal had seen body parts in the river, an indication that there was war upstream. The soldiers took the food supplies and torched the ferry that brought provisions. The villagers around, a good percentage of whom were Dinkas, came and looted the place.

Land mines were scattered across the terrain, making driving a risky venture, but no one thought about this in our panic to escape. Although we were fleeing a lion, that didn't mean we wouldn't be attacked by a cheetah. My people say, *Problems won't leave you alone because you have other problems.* So you face them as you go along. I was learning quickly the importance of quick decision-making during wartime, and also coming to terms with the idea of luck and the philosophy of being protected by the gods, since there was really no science behind the fact that I survived and some of my friends didn't. I had to attribute it to some force bigger than myself, even if I had simplified it to just being lucky, time and again.

We kept driving all the way to Nasir, where we traded our shirts for jars of forest-harvested honey, the only source of food. At that point, I decided to go back home to Akobo, and I lived off the honey for a week as I searched for my mother—both for solace and to care for her. As it turned out, Mum and the kids were already back in Akobo with my father. Once again, my mother gave me one of those tight embraces, which had now become a ritual of ours, what with my risky goings and comings. Sudan was making this sort of life normal, that a child and his mother had to live in perpetual fear of a time when one would leave home, never to come back, and that each time a child returned, it was something to celebrate.

Jangjuol, my old friend from Itang, was in Akobo as well, and he was the same as ever, his body still petite.

JANGJUOL: Ger, where were you for a year?

ME: I was in Baliet in the military barracks with Peter Gatkuoth.

JANGJUOL: Peter Gatkuoth told me you almost got killed there.

ME: It is true, my brother, our Dinka cousins almost finished me off.

JANGJUOL: I am thinking about going back to Ethiopia this year.

ME: Me too! I miss learning in Itang.

JANGJUOL: Want to go swimming?

ME: Let's see if your little body can keep up with me. . . .

To my relief and shock, Peter Gatkuoth showed up in Akobo as well, but he did not look the same. He was bloated, like a fermenting blueberry on the precipice of bursting.

PETER: Everybody is dead.

He passed out right on the spot.

Later, after we'd repeatedly touched sweet honey to his tongue to reinvigorate him and wrapped him in cloth to keep him from getting the chills, even though it was maybe eighty degrees out, through swollen lips and aching limbs he told us the story of how he'd managed to escape.

PETER: I leaped into the water and stayed submerged in the Nile until the shooting subsided. For hours and hours. When I gathered enough strength, I jumped out and started running. But the enemy soldiers pursued and shot at me from their jeep. By some stroke of luck, I outran them.

ME: If it were anyone else, I would have said that was impossible.

PETER: I disappeared into the bushes and walked all the way here, ducking at any sight or sound of people and vehicles. I could never trust anything or anyone.

Senior SPLA officers in Akobo were incensed by Peter's proclamation that everyone was dead. They rumbled as they waited for him to recover, after which they heavily reprimanded him.

SENIOR SPLA OFFICER: What kind of soldier are you? You never say everyone has been killed!

Ah, yes. That good old unwritten rule. The one that allows a messenger to say one day that your brother is alive and well, then the next day, from the other side of his mouth, tell you that he's in fact dead. Always prizing soldier morale over the truth.

But Peter didn't care. In his head, his journey as a soldier was done. They could yell as much as they wanted, but his mind was made up.

By now it was the rainy season. Food was plentiful and the Nile was full with a steady supply of fish. I found myself quickly moving on with life, consoled by a change of circumstance, from hardship to abundance, and surrounded by the love and care of my family. I enjoyed the moment, not knowing what lay ahead. Sudan taught you not to get complacent, not to assume stability. It always had a way of shaking things up and snapping you back to reality.

SAVIORS

I BELIEVE IT WAS LATE 1992 when a group of aid workers arrived in my village of Dengjok, located on the bank of the Pibor River, which meandered into the Nile. They came from Akobo Town, our local administrative center, with a mission to administer vaccinations to children. They arrived on a speedboat, which was exciting since we were more accustomed to seeing slow-moving canoes. The workers quickly addressed a public gathering of villagers, informing us of their mission, and everyone brought their age-appropriate children forward. My father's newest wife, Nyachak, and I took my mother's six-year-old twins, Both and Nyandit, to join the rest of the kids. I left my gun at home, as was customary whenever aid workers came around. The workers loaded all the children into the speedboat and prepared to take them across the quickly flowing river. The speedboat was visibly overloaded, yet there was excitement among the villagers, especially the kids, some of whom were riding on a speedboat for the first time.

My stepmother Nyachak and I stood on the bank with our eyes trained on the twins as they rode off with thirty or so other children. I rolled my pants up to my knees and waved happily, glad that they were going to receive life-saving vaccines, hoping that they would enjoy the ride.

As they rode farther out, Gatwech, whom we knew from back in Itang Camp, where he'd been a driver for the chief of staff and now newly minted SPLA commander William Nyuon Bany Machar, started doing funky moves with the speedboat to impress his audience. Those of us on the riverbank began cheering excitedly, and the kids, whether afraid or ecstatic, kept making similar loud noises. Then, in a split second, while everyone was cheering his antics, the speedboat capsized in the middle of the river, dumping everyone overboard.

From the time the twins were born, I had sworn that I would be like a father to them. As such, I had been present when they started to stand and walk. I had helped teach them how to speak and had even tried to make them swim. In that moment of excitement and confusion as the kids boarded the speedboat, it slipped my mind that Nyandit had always been afraid of water, and that her vehement protestations whenever I put her in a large body of it had made me stop bringing her along with me to the river. It slipped my mind that I should have been on the boat with Nyandit to reassure her.

Suddenly the cheers of excitement now turned into

screams for help and mournful wails. My stepmother and I instantly looked at each other, recognizing that Nyandit didn't know how to swim, and without thinking twice or saying a word, we both dove into the hippo- and crocodile-infested river on a mission to rescue my siblings and any other kids.

I was the first one to arrive at the speedboat. I flipped over every little body I came across—most had already run out of breath—and each time I did so, I found it wasn't Nyandit. I dove into the murky waters of the river over and over again, my fingertips reaching for the bottom, feeling for Nyandit. Nyachak and I were both strong swimmers, but with time, the water overpowered us. Nyachak saved my brother Both, who had managed to hold his breath long enough to be rescued.

I searched for Nyandit for what felt like forever, but after a while, I was too exhausted to continue. All I could think was, in this, the most crucial moment of little Nyandit's life, I had let her down. I had failed to fulfill my deep yearning to care for others, a need—a calling—that would stay with me forever. I started crying and screaming. I jumped right back into the river and spent long minutes underwater, eyes open, looking for her. I decided that if I had to die to find her, then that's what was going to happen. At some point, I felt myself run out of breath and begin to drown. As I tried reaching the surface, I realized how deep I had gone. When I finally came up, I spat out a lot of water, as if I was vomiting. I had literally used up my physical strength.

The people on the riverbank started screaming for me to get out of the water. Nearly comatose, I swam slowly toward the bank, and when I got closer, people pulled me out and laid me on my back. Tears flowed freely from my eyes, my heart completely broken into a thousand pieces. I would never again feel such a sense of failure and defeat. I had let my little sister die.

Two or three other kids had not been found, and at this point, everyone was baying for the blood of Gatwech and the aid workers, who were being guarded across the river. In that moment of chaos, I saw my mother screaming and rolling on the ground. I couldn't take it anymore. I ran home and picked up my gun. When I got back to the river, I started swimming across, slowly, since I was running on fumes. By this time, the whole village had gathered on the bank. Those who hadn't witnessed the events wanted to know the details. The anger blocking my throat and the tears flooding my eyes wouldn't allow me to hold a conversation with anyone. I swam on.

Once I made it across the river, I ran toward the group of elders that had formed a shield around Gatwech and the aid workers. I was ready to open fire and shoot indiscriminately. I didn't care who would die, since the loss of my sister made life not worth living anymore. As I got closer, still crying, a man I respected, Gatluak Ter, came from behind and snatched the gun from me.

GATLUAK TER: Ger, calm down. Ger, it was an accident!

He pinned me down and tried to talk to me, but I wasn't listening. Then a man holding a spear joined the crowd gathering around me, and I sprang up unexpectedly, snatched the spear from his hand, and charged toward Gatwech and the aid workers. Another group of men pinned me down and took the spear away before I could launch it. I had little strength in me to fight and was easily overpowered. All I felt inside was the need for revenge.

The following morning, a group of men went back to the river with a fishing net, and my sister Nyandit's body was recovered. I couldn't go to view it, and when the traditional burial ceremony was being conducted, I stayed away. I was sinking into a deep depression. The one thing I knew was that continuing to stay near the Pibor River made me miserable. The sound of its rushing water was nothing but a constant reminder of my failure to keep Nyandit safe. The next morning, I woke up, packed my few belongings, and headed to the market, where my father was staying. I found him sitting under a tree.

DAD: I have heard.

ME: Gatwech was driving the speedboat. He did it.

By this time, Gatwech had already been confined in a makeshift holding cell. My father, angered, picked up his gun and traced the location. He too wanted to avenge my sister's death, but he was also stopped by the elders. I felt like the shadow of death was following me. I had experienced the death of my brother Oder, then my friends at Baliet, and after I'd escaped from there to come back to Akobo, death had snatched my little sister from me. I felt as though I had to do something dramatic, something that would take me away from this dark cloud that was following me around. I decided I had to leave Akobo, one way or another.

GOOD-BYES

AS THOUGH THE GODS HAD heard my prayers, an escape route out of Akobo presented itself. A couple of weeks after my sister's death, an unusual offer came my way, out of the blue. My friend Jangjuol Biel Jangjuol's first cousin, Paul Jangjuol, was a devout Presbyterian minister, well-known in my town. Paul was twenty-nine and had two prized possessions: an English Bible and a Nuer hymnbook. He told a group of us that he had made it to a refugee camp in Kenya called Walda, where people were being accepted for political-refugee status and sponsorship to immigrate to America, Denmark, and Sweden. He had come all the way back to Akobo to take whichever family members and other local residents wished to make the trip with him. There was no doubt that those who did would risk their lives, because it involved a long trek to Ethiopia: back to Itang, then on to Addis Ababa, with no guarantee of safety.

I told myself I had already done these risky expeditions

countless times before. And besides, I did not feel I was truly alive in Akobo, and so I had to go and find something new. What I didn't realize at fourteen was that I could leave Akobo, but I could never block out the memories of violence—like those of my sister's death and my life as a soldier. They would forever haunt me, no matter how far away I traveled or how many years I spent without going back.

ME: Mum, I have to leave again. I want to go back to Ethiopia and try to go to school.

I was lying to her because I didn't want her to worry that I was taking a long, uncertain journey to an unknown place and future. I sensed, however, that she knew my spirit had left this place. She too seemed to have lost her ability to feel, so she understood. Nyandit's tragic death had snatched something out of every one of us.

MUM: I have no objection, my son. Do what you have to do.

ME: Thank you.

MUM: It's even better if you go. Staying around here is just going to get you hurt or killed for no reason.

ME: You understand.

MUM: We have a relative who lives along the path you will take toward Ethiopia. He is caring for a family cow. Tell him you have my permission to take it, then sell it. Give the money to Paul to ensure your safe passage to the refugee camp in Kenya and get your education, once and for all.

ME: Thanks, Mum. In case things get difficult, please remember to seek help from Uncle Reat.

I knew my father was not one to be counted on at such times, since he was so often preoccupied by other things. But Uncle Reat was a dependable hand. He had never left Akobo, no matter how dire the security situation had gotten. He always tilled the land and had just enough to feed himself and those around him, no matter how bad the weather was. He wouldn't let the sister who had raised him starve alongside her kids under his watch. My little brothers Gok and Both and my sister Nyakuar would stay behind with my stepmother Nyachak, who had two children by this time. She would also keep an eye on my mother.

I didn't want my father to know I was leaving, because he would try to stop me. And I didn't tell my mother I had no intention of stopping. Mum packed two heavy bags of maize for me.

ME: Nyakuar, would you please help me carry one?

My mother gave me her last blessings, putting her frail hands on my head and whispering traditional prayers. She had aged a thousand years from the gastrointestinal problems for which she could not get treatment.

MUM: May my son travel peacefully. Nothing is going to happen to you as long as I am still in this universe. Go!

With tears flowing down my cheeks, I said good-bye to my mother, not sure when, or if, I would ever see her again. It seemed as though I had spent half my life saying good-bye to her. I made a promise to myself that I would return someday to help her, as she had helped me. I then set forth with Nyakuar, who believed we had been sent to deliver the maize to a relative's home. I bid farewell to Akobo, feeling this departure had come none too soon.

Nyakuar and I walked side by side, and I knew the route because I had followed it coming from Itang. Paul had not invited me to join the group directly, but since he had made a public call in Akobo, I figured he wouldn't turn me away. He was a man of God, after all, and I hadn't come empty-handed. We soon got to the village where Paul's group was taking a rest, and here I relayed the news to Nyakuar with tears in my eyes.

ME: I must take this maize off you and send you back home. I am not going with you.

Nyakuar, stoic as ever, didn't blink or lose her cool.

NYAKUAR: There's nowhere in this world where people don't die, Ger. If it's meant for you to go to school, you go. But if you die along the way, like Nyandit just did, know that that's how everybody dies in this country anyway.

My little sister's words almost broke me, but seeing her unfazed gave me the strength to carry on with the journey. I was doing this not just for myself, but for all of us, to prove that there was a better tomorrow lying somewhere on the horizon. I bid Nyakuar an emotional good-bye, with a tight embrace. I took the maize and started running after Paul's group. Nyakuar stood there, her gaze trained on the vista far away, watching me disappear, soaking up one last look at me before the world swallowed me whole. I turned around and waved a final good-bye, still crying, and ran farther into uncertainty. When I caught up with Paul, his first reaction was disbelief.

PAUL: Ger, is that you? I cannot believe Thabach has allowed you to come. Your father is a difficult man.

ME: I came with my mother's blessings.

I gave Paul all I owned—for pay or barter—and told him I was in. When we got to my relative's home, he didn't object to me taking that cow. I had bought myself a one-way ticket out of Sudan.

With Paul were his thirteen-year-old brother, Both; his cousins Nyakume and Nyangile, who were sisters; and their brother, my friend Jangjuol. There were about six other boys on the trip. My friend Peter Gatkuoth had come along with us this far, but he wasn't yet ready to leave Akobo, and so Jangjuol and I hugged him good-bye. This felt like good-bye forever, which pained me greatly. But it was also good riddance to my past. And I needed my past behind me.

As we started moving toward Ethiopia, Jangjuol and I stayed behind the pack and swore that we would make it to America if it was the last thing we did. All we knew about the country was that it was a military power, that Michael Jackson was from there, that my father's brother, the highly respected professor Wal Duany, lived there, and that we had always thought all airplanes came from there. As one passed overhead, we shouted.

ME AND JANGJUOL: *Mericama! Mericama!*

MAKING THE CUT

WE TOOK THE DANGEROUS WALK west, across southern Sudan, over the Ethiopian border, and finally got back to Itang. The camp looked more or less the same, though sparsely populated following our last mass exodus. There wasn't any trace of an SPLA presence. The Ethiopians seemed to have been keeping a closer eye on things now, their government granting residence to Sudanese refugees but not to any SPLA members.

PAUL: Once we get to Gambella, we will pay truck drivers to smuggle us through Ethiopia into Kenya. It will take days, and means switching from one truck to another.

ME: I've smuggled myself on trucks many times. This will be a piece of cake.

PAUL: If only it were that easy. We won't have food or water for many hours at a time. Maybe days. And armed military personnel could discover us at any of the checkpoints along the way. Now is the time to speak up if this is not for you.

We all stood there in silence. Paul looked out of the corner of his eye to see if anyone was wavering. But despite his firm warnings, we all decided to forge ahead.

Regardless of the rough terrain and inadequate rest, the fact that we were on the move toward someplace hopeful invigorated us. Once at Gambella, I saw light-skinned men with curly hair and rusty front teeth chewing khat—the color of their teeth a side effect of drinking excessively strong coffee. Paul spoke Amharic to a number of truck drivers, negotiating a fee for us to get to Gore, our next stop. He came back bearing sad news.

PAUL: They want more money than we have. We can only afford the trip if I send one or two of you back to Sudan.

He addressed each one of us separately, giving reasons why we were or weren't eligible to continue with the journey.

PAUL: Ger, your mother sacrificed a cow for you to come on this journey. We've sold the cow and that money will be useful to us. For this reason, you will come with us.

After Paul was done reassuring me, I stayed quiet and still, maintaining sympathetic eye contact with him, lest he change his mind. I wanted to exclaim in relief but didn't, knowing that someone, at least one of us, had to go back. I held my peace so I wouldn't appear to be gloating.

PAUL: Jangjuol, we can't send your sisters Nyangile and Nyakume back. So, for that reason, you will have to go home. But one day we will find a way to get you out of Sudan.

Everyone turned around to look at Jangjuol's crestfallen face. He tried not to show his anguish.

PAUL: If you get back home, please tell everyone we have made it this far.

If.
That was the first time I had ever seen my usually animated friend speechless. I will never forget the deflated look on Jangjuol's face as we boarded the cargo truck the next morning. I imagined him making the journey back to Sudan alone and wanted to tell him it wasn't my fault that he hadn't made the cut, that I would opt out and let him take my place. But it wasn't true.

We were all silent during the journey across the mountainous Ethiopian countryside, with its narrow roads meandering to and fro, its steep slopes and sloppy terrain.

We got to Gore late at night, and the chilly weather was unbearable to people coming from hot Sudan. Paul got us some Ethiopian food: injera, with a tasty sauce, which was our only meal for the day. He then rented a room for the night. The entire group crowded inside, some squeezing on the bed, others spreading themselves on a mat on the floor. What mattered was that we had a roof over our heads and that we were moving away from Sudan.

The weather remained torturous the following morning, and we hadn't brought along any heavy clothing. Every one of us was shivering. Paul got us some tea, sold on the streets, after which we made our way to the main bus park in Gore.

BYSTANDERS: Chinkila! Chinkila! Chinkila!

Different groups of Ethiopians heckled us as we walked by, calling us a degrading term that meant "dark-skinned." We were all as dark-skinned as a Sudanese could get, and I was quietly fuming. Paul, knowing I had once been an AK-47-carrying young man who had both shot and been shot at, quickly intervened. He spoke to the group of us, but looked at me specifically.

PAUL: Don't mind them. We still have a long journey ahead of us. Don't get distracted.

Paul knew as well as I did that to a Nuer man, nothing mattered more than his sense of self-worth, his dignity and that of his family. In this case, the people I was traveling with were my family. Though I was still in my teens, I was already acting like a man—leaving home and going on long treks in search of a livelihood, always ready to defend my honor. After Paul's intervention, I swallowed my anger and kept moving.

From Gore, we took another cargo truck to Jimma, the most advanced and picturesque urban space I had ever seen. It was much bigger than Malakal, with wider, more populous streets. I tried counting the number of trucks I came across and quickly lost track. There were endless shops, and I could manage to store only a fraction of all this in my mind. I took that as my cue to surrender to a new reality. Maybe these were the sorts of places I would encounter from now on, places with a vibrant street life, where everyone seemed to mind their own business.

To me, this looked like how proper human beings should live, with shops well stocked with supplies. Back home, no matter how much food there was in a town or an SPLA camp, you knew war would break out and it would be back to square one: starvation. If anything were to happen to me at this point in our journey, I could at least say that I saw Jimma with my own two eyes and felt like I had made it in life. I kept repeating this to myself, powering myself further. No turning back, no matter what.

That night, we slept in a rented room much smaller than the one we shared in Gore.

PAUL: From here on, things are going to get expensive. City life is very costly, and so we'll make do with only what we can afford.

Paul had bought us flip-flops and a few clothes in Gambella, but it was going to take more than some new clothing to make us look like anything resembling urban dwellers.

I stayed up through the night imagining what the bus ride from Jimma to Addis Ababa, Ethiopia's capital, would feel like; wondering whether I would be allowed to sit on the soft seats that I guessed were reserved for adults who cleaned up nicely; worrying that Paul would have to turn more of us back if we couldn't afford the cost of the ride for the entire group. I tossed and turned the whole night.

The following morning, Paul told us his strategy for the trip.

PAUL: I have timed the duration of the trip from here to Addis Ababa. We must travel after midnight so that we get to Addis in the morning. That way, we won't need to pay for accommodation. We'll proceed to the Kenyan border right away.

Late that night, he took us to the bus station, where we boarded the most comfortable means of transport I had ever taken. The bus had plush seats and traditional Ethiopian music, which sounded like Arabic music from Khartoum, playing from little speakers mounted on the ceiling. All these things were a spectacle to me, and much as I presented a calm exterior, I remained tense and restless, trying to take everything in.

I chose a window seat so I could look out and experience the Ethiopian countryside, even in the dead of night. To my pleasant surprise, everyone, young and old, had their own seat on the bus. I tried to stay awake throughout the journey, despite my overwhelming exhaustion, and only knew I'd lost that battle when I woke upon arrival in Addis Ababa the following morning.

HOSPITALITY

AS SOON AS WE DISEMBARKED, Paul pulled me aside.

PAUL: I can take you to see your cousin Gasim Gam.

ME: That would be great.

After Oder had left for the SPLA front line, Gasim had moved to the Ethiopian capital, avoiding SPLA fighting duty, possibly taking the same advice Oder had given me: get an education, do not let being a soldier be your highest aspiration in life. Once in Addis Ababa, Gasim had enrolled in school and was now struggling through college.

We found Gasim living in pretty deplorable conditions, even by Sudanese village standards. It was a tiny, congested, unkempt house with poor ventilation. Back in Akobo, the huts were clean and spacious, at least, well ventilated with adequate distance between them, complete with open fields used as playgrounds for children. Where Gasim lived was a congregation of little rooms with limited natural lighting, the general surroundings reeking of poor sanitation.

Upon seeing us at his door that early in the morning, Gasim started oscillating between excitement and despair: happy to see us but regretting that he had nothing to offer us, like breakfast.

I understood how difficult things must have been for him, having had no relatives in Addis Ababa and being dependent on handouts from generous well-wishers. A tiny bed with a worn-out mattress and a reading table were all he had, but whatever Gasim lacked in material things, he made up for in good cheer and a resilient spirit. He never wallowed in self-pity, no matter how dire his circumstances. He was a true southern Sudanese.

PAUL: Gasim, sorry to ambush you so early in the morning. I have brought you guests.

In African culture, receiving guests, including (and especially) unannounced ones, is considered a blessing, a sign that the ancestors have appointed you to be host of your relatives with pride and kindness. From that, more good tidings are to come your way.

GASIM: Oh, my people. You are very much welcome. Look at Ger, all grown up. Ger, how is everyone back home?

ME: Everyone is fine, Gasim, but things are still dire. I've left to try to get an education.

Gasim knew that Nyandit had passed away, but we did not dwell on that or on the death of his uncle Keep due to famine. We Sudanese do not dwell on death. If we did, we'd be in a perpetual state of mourning. Instead, we move on with life.

GASIM: As you can see from my example, it's not going to be easy. But that's the right decision.

I found the cold in Ethiopia unbearable, and so I asked Gasim for an extra item of clothing.

GASIM: I'm sorry, Ger, but I haven't received any money lately and have no extra clothing. The only thing I can offer you is that blue T-shirt over there. You can have it if you like it.

The T-shirt was dirty and sticky with lice, but I had no choice. I glanced at Paul before picking it up, then smiled appreciatively at my cousin.

Later that evening, we headed by bus to the Kenyan border. We got off on the Ethiopian side at a small shopping center, where we joined a group of Ethiopians trying to sneak into Kenya. We couldn't go through the official border point and face the Kenyan and Ethiopian immigration officials since none of us had proper travel documents. The alternate route was through a heavily forested mountainous terrain, but we couldn't be seen heading through there as a group, because that would make it obvious we were sneaking in. Paul devised another plan.

PAUL: We are going to walk toward the forest one by one. The most we can risk is two people moving together. Once you get there, just keep walking.

We started trickling into the trees at around two p.m. After walking for almost half an hour, we assembled at the foot of a mountain for a quick head count to ensure everyone had made it that far. We had now formed a joint climbing party with the Ethiopians, our fates intertwined. There were no clear footpaths up the mountain, yet it seemed like those leading the pack, Paul and others, had a general sense of the direction we were going. Throughout the climb, monkeys residing in the mountain kept making noises, as if to alert us to their presence.

There was talk within the group that Ethiopian and Somali rebels sometimes took cover in the mountains, and for this reason we tried to walk as quietly as we could. If anyone wanted to pass along a message within the group, they would gesture for everyone to gather around. No shouting was permitted. The Ethiopians journeying with us told us a group of Sudanese escapees had been ambushed and killed in the forest a fortnight earlier.

We got to the mountaintop after dark and rested briefly before starting downhill. I kept looking at Nyangile and Nyakume, wondering how taxing this must be for them. I was tired and thirsty, but this type of journey had become a kind of adventure for me. I had learned never to dwell on the difficulties but always to keep my mind focused on the destination. In that way, immediate suffering faded.

By the time the sun came out, after a number of stopovers and quick naps, we found ourselves on the Kenyan side of the border. I once again felt like I was moving toward my future against all odds. Our first human contact was with Turkana men and women, tall, skinny, and dark, just like the Sudanese. We came to a traditional homestead at the bottom of the mountain, where a man was lying down next to a cattle kraal, resting his head on a tiny three-legged stool. He rose to his feet upon seeing us. Instead of questioning us, he ushered us into his homestead, possibly aware we'd had a long night trekking through the forest.

Paul whispered to us as we went.

PAUL: They are good people. Don't panic or show any resistance.

There was a language barrier, but somehow the Ethiopians managed to ask the man if he could get us some drinking water. The man shouted something, and a woman came from farther inside the house. She shook our hands, after which she took a traditional pot and vanished for ten or so minutes, returning with water. She then got a plastic jar from one of the mud houses for us to use as a drinking vessel. We each gulped down water before passing the jar on to the next person. Paul made what looked like an attempt to ask for directions. The man spoke and gestured, and Paul seemed to understand. We bid the man and woman farewell and headed toward Walda.

It took us another six hours to get to the refugee camp. That year, drought had killed a lot of livestock—camels, cows, and goats. In Walda there were hundreds of southern Sudanese but also hundreds of thousands of refugees from the Ethiopian civil war. This new life in the camp consisted of us sitting around, scrounging, and squabbling over food or perceived slights. I met Paul's friend Gatluak Riek, who was, I sensed immediately, someone I could learn from— not only had he received a proper education in Nairobi, but all the girls in the camp said he had the nicest smile they had ever seen. Gatluak Riek further convinced me that I needed to go to America.

As fate would have it, I spotted Lual Nyang, my English-speaking friend from Itang, who'd kept an eye out for me there since I tended to get into fights. Lual had grown a big Afro with a perfect hairline, like the comedian Steve Harvey's in the 1990s.

As 1993 turned to 1994, we all moved camp to Ifo, in Garissa County, Kenya. This was the first time I'd ever seen so many white people: they were donors or "high-profile" supporters of the UN. Later on, I learned that their mission was to assess the camp in order to build a school and also a treatment center for children, since so many lacked health care and proper diets. We didn't have any intimate interaction with them because there was tight security, but we just found them fascinating.

Lual and I would venture off into the bushes to squat and pee. That was when we had this exchange:

LUAL: Man, we gotta stick together in this camp. Because any day we could be in America, Canada, or a Scandinavian country like Denmark or Norway.

ME: Maybe we'd grow old there. Sometimes I wonder if that means we won't ever be able to come home again. If we'll be stranded in some European country. I'm already homesick. I miss my family.

LUAL: We are going to be okay, Ger.

ME: *Nyajuri!*

LUAL: *Nyajuri!!!*

"*Nyajuri*" means "togetherness under one roof" and signified our brotherhood.

We waited for our destinies to be handed to us, since it seemed all we could do as refugees was wait. We met a boy, Thomas Kutey, who had a huge family and resided in Kenya's capital, Nairobi, because his father was an educator and a politician. That's where and how he had learned to speak proper English and Swahili. He had never lived in a refugee camp, but when he came to Ifo for a visit, we somehow clicked and became friends.

Most of the time, Lual and I hung out with a boy named Nhial, whom we called Mini Leg because he was so short, and Mai, a kinky-haired and angry boy who bore the traditional Nuer warrior scars on his face. We played soccer in the dusty field by ourselves, collected firewood, and tried to keep one another laughing while standing in line to receive our UN food rations.

Things got tense when Nhial got a girl pregnant. The girl's brothers stormed through camp, threatening to beat up anyone who was a friend of Nhial's. That put a target directly on my back. Not just from them, but also from Paul!

PAUL: YOU KNEW ABOUT THIS, GER? HOW COULD YOU LET THIS HAPPEN? YOU ARE A BAD INFLUENCE!

I clearly had nothing to do with Nhial and the girl's actions, but Paul wouldn't hear it. This created a lot of tension between me and Paul, which we eventually settled as a family, but it left a bad taste in my mouth—one that would build up, like bile, and come roaring back years later.

Despite all that drama, my friends and I continued to meet, play, and speak of America—the dream of having our choice of different pants and shirts to dress in, and speaking English perfectly without any African accents. The word "America" itself became imbued with so many meanings and possibilities, most of them vague, like the remnants of a dream, but all infused with hope. Every week, we hoped to see our names printed on the UNHCR chalkboard, which would signify that we were finally scheduled to leave the camp. And so we waited.

COMING TO AMERICA

EACH MORNING, I WOULD CHECK the chalkboard outside the UNHCR building in Ifo. It would sometimes take me half an hour to get there, but all I could think about was the prospect of making it to America. Up the stairs, through the corridors, I'd stop in front of the board and read the name of every person on the list to make certain I didn't miss mine. On March 7, 1994, I headed up those steps and scanned that board like any other day, poring over dozens of names, when my heart leaped into my throat. There it WAS: GABRIEL GER THABACH DUANY. My name. Typed up on an old-school typewriter. I spelled it out in my head again and again, making sure I'd read it right. But I had. It felt, I imagine, like winning a Mega Millions lottery. I'm not sure when I started breathing or walking again, but I somehow made it home, dazed and dreaming of how my life would change. How everything would now be better. How there would be food, and money, and education, and opportunity there for the taking. How I could put war behind me. How the battles I fought, inside and out, would end, and I would have peace. Finally, there would be peace.

Within three days, we were relocated to a camp in Ruiru for our medical checks. I couldn't sleep at night with all the adrenaline pulsing through my body, penetrating my soul. I would finally step foot on American soil. And then the guilt and sadness set in. What would happen to my family? How could I be happy when I'd be leaving them behind— the people who loved me and fought for me. Even died for me. Would I see them again in this lifetime if I crossed the Mediterranean Sea, if I traversed the Atlantic? Was I ungrateful in wanting to leave?

As I drifted off, Oder appeared in my mind, insisting that I make something of myself. I whispered aloud, "Why not risk it all? What's the worst thing that could happen if I go? I already know what will happen if I stay." And then I thought about what Nyakuar told me as we parted ways and said our good-byes: *There's nowhere in this world where people don't die.* Words to live by. She told me, *Go find yourself some opportunity in a strange land.* That advice keeps me going to this day.

The night before we left for the States, Lual came by with a package.

LUAL: This is for you, so you can fit in as soon as you arrive. That is, if your dark skin and eight-foot-tall height don't give you away first.

I unwrapped the stiff brown paper and found a pair of blue jeans inside! They were his old but still good-looking Levi's, with a sewed-on patch of the American flag. I pulled off my shorts and tried them on right away. Instantly I was filled with excitement. I decided to sleep in my new jeans for two reasons: one, so I would be certain not to forget them, and two, so I'd arrive in America already looking the part.

Once at Jomo Kenyatta International Airport in Nairobi, we went through immigration and proceeded to join other passengers in the waiting area. When it was time to board, we walked toward a plane that appeared big enough to transport an entire village of hundreds of people. I never imagined airplanes, which looked like small birds as they passed over our heads, could be this enormous. We ascended the metal stairs, and the moment we got inside, I started shivering, my skin bubbling up with goose pimples from the steep drop in temperature. The entire interior was smooth, and the flight attendants showed us to our seats. None of us had any idea what to do with the little screens in front of us.

I tried to keep my composure and didn't dare touch a thing. I didn't want to risk messing things up and getting thrown off our flight. America now seemed like a real place, both so close I could feel its energy in my bones and so far away: one slipup or tap on the shoulder from a soldier could end my dream—my life—in an instant.

Our plane was bursting with Sudanese, Somalis, and Ethiopians, each one of whom looked as lost as we were. Most likely refugees like ourselves.

ANNOUNCEMENT: Ladies and gentlemen, welcome aboard Lufthansa flight 598, with service from Nairobi to Frankfurt. We ask that you fasten your seat belts at this time and secure your baggage underneath your seat or in the overhead compartment. Thank you for choosing Lufthansa German Airlines. Enjoy your flight!

Men and women dressed in uniforms walked the aisle, checking that everyone had belted up and that the luggage compartment was locked. After a few more announcements from the faceless voice, the plane started moving, and I felt a mixture of joy and sadness.

ME: Oh, God, may we travel to this new foreign land peacefully, and may our friends in camps follow us in peace. Amen-Rah.

I thought of my mother, brothers, and sisters in Akobo. I promised myself I would never forget where I came from, and that once I made it in America, I would come back home and uplift my family.

In a bit, the wheels of the mammoth bird moved across the tarmac, and as it gained momentum, it catapulted us through time and space to another world, our fate no longer in our own hands.

I looked around and saw other passengers relaxed into their seats, and decided to do just as they did. I stretched my legs, laid my head back, and tried to enjoy the ride, though the adrenaline rush, mixed with nervousness, was not cooperating. I saw clouds in close proximity and wondered whether this was what they meant in our Bible school classes when they said a cloud took Jesus up out of sight, toward heaven. I wondered if maybe America was closer to heaven, given that Sudan, with all the hunger and suffering, would logically have to be much farther away.

FLIGHT ATTENDANT: Hello, sir. We are serving curried beef for dinner tonight.

The thought of being served a meal by a white person blew my mind. At Ifo, they had been demigods in our eyes, working for the United Nations and having the power to change our lives with a mere stroke of the pen. I imagined these hostesses either owned this airplane or were highly paid employees of the United Nations, tasked with transporting us to America.

The food, packaged in tiny portions, looked strange. I slowly opened each pack, and the only two things that looked familiar were milk and meat, but I couldn't understand why it was packed in such tiny quantities. Everyone around me was busy eating, and so I followed suit. Then, with help, I made my seat recline, and I closed my eyes to enjoy an unusually unburdened slumber.

First stop: Frankfurt.

We were all commanded to get off the plane. I was used to the fits and starts, detours and zigzags that came with travel and, more specifically, fleeing to safety. So we created yet another kind of caravan of people and trekked from one side of the airport to the other in order to get to our next gate. It was on this excursion that I witnessed one of the most astonishing sights I had ever seen in my life: the escalator. It scared virtually every last one of us.

PAUL: Stay calm. Calm down. Put one foot on the flat surface and get your other foot on it right after. Watch. Like this.

He rode up the escalator, then came back down again, to show us how it was done and to give the first child the courage to take the leap of faith. Then came my turn.

PAUL: Do not panic, Ger. It is easier than it appears. You will enjoy it once you're on it.

That escalator ride convinced me we were in the vicinity of heaven, since I couldn't understand how this could be a part of people's everyday lives. I couldn't see dust or dirt anywhere, not a single tree or even a bird, yet I could see my reflection almost everywhere I looked. The idea of heaven was unfolding right in front of my eyes. We got to a waiting area where all kinds of people were moving in and out. Screens with words and images running up and down littered the walls, and my little education at the refugee camps couldn't come to my aid. In time, we heard it— a name I recognized since Paul had said it'd be our first stop in America.

ANNOUNCEMENT: Now boarding on Delta: Frankfurt to New York.

The airplane was as huge as the one we had boarded from Nairobi, and everything inside looked similar. Now that I had been on an airplane before, I decided that I wouldn't show my naivete again. I feigned confidence as I went up the stairs to board, and once inside, I acted nonchalant.

On the other hand, Both, Paul's younger brother, couldn't hide his fascination. I was waiting for the moment he would touch something and mess it up, but before that happened, I drifted off once more. At the tail end of another extended nap, I sensed the plane descending and opened my eyes as its wheels touched the runway at JFK International Airport. On the other side of the porthole window was a sea of lights a hundred times the candescence of those I'd glimpsed in Nairobi. When we entered the terminal from the Jetway, I stopped in my tracks. Here was the largest number of people I'd ever witnessed in one place, people of different nationalities pulling suitcases every which way. Paul spun in a circle, trying to locate our connecting flight, then did a quick, silent head count of our group.

PAUL: Where is Both? Ger, Nyakume, where is Both?

Paul got anxious and angry. Intent on not losing anyone else, we searched for him as a group for close to half an hour, after which he emerged from the lavatory. Paul yanked him to his side and gave him and us a quick dressing-down.

PAUL: Next time any of you sees fit to run off, keep running.

We had a connecting flight to make but didn't know how to find it, and no one was able to help us when we asked. Finally, Paul handed someone our tickets.

PAUL: Dess Moh-ee-ness?

The gentleman took one look, checked the airport screens, and spotted our flight.

GENTLEMAN: That one right there. To Des Moines, Iowa.

Paul had been mispronouncing the name, leaving everyone else he'd asked confused.

PAUL: Thank you.

We rushed to the boarding gate, got helped into the plane by airport staffers, and were off on our last leg to our final destination. For now.

WELCOME WAGON

TWO OF PAUL'S SUDANESE FRIENDS, James Bol Both and Koang Toang, who had settled in America in the '90s and had made plans for us to get here through the sponsorship of the Lutheran Church, received us at the airport. They showed up in their vehicles, a 1993 red Pontiac Grand Am and a white two-door Ford Mustang, which felt surreal, seeing people with my skin color living the American dream. Bol and Koang embraced us, and watching them mingle freely with white people gave me a sense of absolute confidence—that, and my blue jeans from Lual. I felt I could be them if everything went according to plan.

JAMES BOL AND KOANG: *Maalę! Maalę! Maalę!*

Hearing my native language in this very white world made me light-headed; I wasn't sure what was real. Bol and Koang were accompanied by Man Mark, an old white

Lutheran woman, who was in effect our host. According to Nuer culture, older women are called by their sons' names. That's how we came to call her Man Mark, meaning "mother of Mark" in Nuer.

Koang shared an apartment with Bol, Bol's wife, and their two kids. Bol's wife had prepared a huge feast for us, which was laid out on the dining room table. Everyone had their own plate—something I had never experienced—and we all served ourselves to our satisfaction. For the first time in my life, I ate as much as I could. I couldn't believe I was walking away from a table that was still full of food, but I was too stuffed to be able to speak much.

JAMES BOL: Guys, eat. You know, in America you have to eat as much as you want.

ME: I have had enough to eat, Bol. Could I please take a bath?

JAMES BOL: Yes, Ger. You will all take a shower before going to bed.

I got to shower first. Bol gave me a clean towel, which I was afraid to use, thinking I would make it too dirty. He took me to a bathroom inside the house, something else I had never experienced, and showed me the hot- and cold-water taps. I had only ever bathed in rivers, and only used a bathroom at the refugee holding place in Nairobi before making the journey to America. What fascinated me most was that water was running freely from the shower, disappearing into a little hole in the floor.

The moment I opened the taps, having forgotten which was for cold and which was for hot, scalding water came down at me with high pressure, burning my skin. I reached for the tap but couldn't master how to close it, and the water burned me more.

ME: Koang! Please come help me. Someone please come help me!

I screamed as loud as I could from the shower. Koang ran into the bathroom and found me naked, scared, and burning.

KOANG: Oh, Ger. I'm so sorry. Let me balance out the water for you so that it isn't too hot.

I kept the water running when I exited the shower so the next person would not suffer the same fate as I.

That was my introduction to America: a scalding. Burned by water, this time literally. It added insult to injury because even here, it seemed, there was no escaping the trauma and reminders of my past.

PART III

MISINTERPRETERS

WHEN EACH OF US WAS clean, Bol and Koang showed us to two bedrooms that Paul, Nyakume, Both, and I would occupy—Both and I in one, Paul and Nyakume in the other. There were two huge beds, and everyone had their own blanket. The floor was carpeted and I felt like lying down there. I had slept on worse surfaces before, and the bed seemed to me like a compact mattress on a giant bed.

The following morning, we had tea, bread, eggs, and meaty strips I later learned were bacon. I supposed this was our meal for the day and was surprised to notice I had suddenly lost my appetite for food. Later that day, we went to the grocery store, where Bol and Koang filled a trolley cart with meats, fruits, vegetables, and other supplies. I was overwhelmed, especially by the amount of meat on display in the store, and what ran through my mind was that the owner of the herd of cattle must have suffered a huge loss.

We pushed the trolley to the cashier, where the bill was paid, but to my surprise, Bol and Koang started walking away, leaving the food behind. I ran after them.

ME: Koang, you guys have forgotten the things you paid for back there!

KOANG: Oh, Ger, don't worry. Those will be brought to the car.

Koang laughed at my naivete. I realized I had a lot to learn to properly fit into the American way of life. My blue jeans were not cutting it.

A week or so later, Paul, Both, Nyakume, and I moved into a two-bedroom apartment in what looked like an African American neighborhood. Both and I went to North High School with other Sudanese refugees, including Gajaak Gatluak, who spoke Thok Naath, the Nuer language, with an eastern Nuer accent; the coolheaded William Deng; Wu-Chan Toang, who was our host Koang's brother; and two sisters named Dukan Bel and Char Bel.

Wu-Chan, red-eyed, wore a bandanna, dressed in baggy jeans, and spoke slang to the African American students, showing us that he belonged. William Deng, on the other hand, only ever nodded in recognition whenever he encountered his African American classmates. The two were the closest we came to interacting with actual Americans, and they always joked about us Sudanese refugees and our ways.

WU-CHAN: When homies say, "What's up?" just make sure you reply by bobbing your head. That's how we do it around here.

WILLIAM DENG: And please act like you've been here before. Don't embarrass yourself by saying "What?" anytime you don't know what's going on.

We would walk to the cafeteria together at lunchtime, and not being well accustomed to what was on offer on the menu, we'd all watch either William Deng or Wu-Chan and see what he did.

WU-CHAN: Yeah, um, gimme a chicken leg and some macaroni.

ME: Chicken leg and macaroni.

BOTH: Chicken leg. Macaroni.

Whatever Wu-Chan or William Deng picked for lunch was what we would all pick. Then, after every meal, we'd tell refugee jokes among ourselves, about how we all moved together like sheep and copied what the first person did.

WILLIAM DENG: Yo, I'm gonna jump off the capitol building. Who's with me?

ME AND BOTH: I am!

Both made friends with the Americans easily and learned everything at a quicker pace than any of the rest of us. He was likable and outgoing, joining all kinds of groups. In the Sudanese community, word was that Both had no shame in his game. He was the first to know the names in English of all the foods in the cafeteria and came boasting to me.

BOTH: This is a burger. This is lettuce. This is cheese.

ME: How do you know this?

BOTH: My friend over there told me.

On some days, Both would enter our apartment and start naming things.

BOTH: Hey, Ger. This is a refrigerator. This here is a freezer.

I would stand there acting uninterested, pretending that I too knew what he was talking about. I wasn't and I didn't.

Twice a week, a group of us new immigrants, most of whom were refugees from across the world—Somalia, Bosnia, Vietnam, Ethiopia, Sudan, Afghanistan—attended evening classes at a facility in downtown Des Moines, where Mr. Anderson, a tall, gentle white man with gray hair, taught us English as a second language. We clustered in groups of students with shared nationalities, almost as though it was safe here not to assimilate or fit in, even though the goal of learning English was to do the opposite. Very confusing!

PRISONER

DURING MY FIRST YEAR IN high school, in the fall of 1994, I experienced extreme culture shock. I expected to be allowed to work and earn money to send back home, but since I was only sixteen, I had to learn to behave like an American adolescent. Being told what to do and when, and responding to the bell in school like an automaton, made no sense to me. I had been walking the earth independently since I was twelve and had no idea how to become a child again.

Paul was often on my case about attending church and living a pious life. But I'd been through too much—seen and heard of too many people killing in the name of God—to believe that this person had any better understanding of what God wanted from me than I did myself. He had this annoying habit of lecturing me—all of us, actually—and conducting long, boring family interventions to talk about our problems, constantly quoting the Bible, not understanding that I didn't want to talk. Couldn't talk. Not to him. Not to anyone.

This new world often defied my comprehension—gleaming glass towers, paved roads filled with sparkling new cars, the distinct absence of AK-47 fire. However, I quickly discovered a new kind of assault, not deadly to the body but destructive to the mind. Some of my classmates were very cruel, and insults and racist comments flew toward me like iron filings to a magnet. Initially, I was ignorant to what was racist and what wasn't, since I hadn't imagined that my skin color, much as it was different, would be an issue, especially since the majority of my schoolmates were African Americans, whose skin colors weren't so different from mine, even though I was darker. As black as ebony.

I noticed early on some complexities of racial identity in America, including with colorism within the black community. African Americans looked down on Africans—we knew nothing about America—and expressed mild disdain for or curiosity about people from the Caribbean. Caribbean people looked down on African Americans—they considered them uncivilized—and admired Africans because we were from the motherland. And then we Africans just tried to fit in, although, of course, we had our different ethnicities and nationalities that kept us apart (Nuer versus Dinka, Sudanese versus Somali). Outside of all this were the white people. Then, as now, in Des Moines as well as in Sudan, lighter complexions signaled easier times.

What often happened in the boys' locker room before phys ed, or while on the basketball court, was that some

African American kid, who clearly had no idea where I came from or what I'd been through, would shout a slur at me.

One time, they decided they were going to fight me at three p.m. in the locker room.

KID: African booty scratcher!

I was silent. He came up behind me and brushed against me, trying to get me to react. So I did. I stood up and pushed him hard. And then a different kid started punching me from the back. It was a rumble in the locker room.

In truth, these kids were really pushing it. I'd been to war and survived it. Sometimes war still raged in my mind. I was not looking to make enemies, but they were making enemies of me, something I would not have advised.

These fights at school further drove a wedge between Paul and me, since to him I was a reckless former child soldier who was refusing to reform to his ways. I was still a boy with no idea how to operate with the self-control and decorum required in America, but racism permeated my life in Des Moines much more than ever before. I struggled to learn how to confront it without tearing my opponents apart, which, unbeknownst to them, I knew how to do—though perhaps not without ruining my own life in the process.

I also had a problem following the school schedule, and a girl named Kimberly, who seemed to like me a lot, helped me understand when I needed to be where. My other big battle was algebra, which I totally couldn't comprehend.

Ms. Johnson, a blond woman who taught us math and had developed a liking for me, went out of her way to try to help me improve my grades. It was not just that I was learning a new language, lifestyle, and worldview. I was also suffering from post-traumatic stress disorder, like so many refugees do. So few, including me, knew what that was or how to deal with it, so we suffered inside our own heads and hearts in silence, without the words or a universal language to describe our torment.

Those nights that first year were bad: often sleepless, my eyes dry from too much blinking or wet from too much quiet crying. When my lids would finally close and I'd slip into sleep, it wasn't dreams that came but chaotic nightmares without end. I shouted in Nuer, thrashed about, feeling that I was back on the front lines, my finger on the trigger, ready for a snapping twig to mean my death or someone else's. America felt lonely. I felt trapped, a prisoner, and unable to fully come to grips with its expectations, with working for grades in school when all I'd ever wanted was to know how to read and write. It seemed like too much pressure.

I worried about Mum too, and hoped she would hear, through that reliable refugee grapevine—the same whisper network that passed along my father's instructions as well as news of my brother Oder's death—that I had safely made it to America. The idea that she might think me dead, not that long after Nyandit had been killed, also haunted me. However, money was of little use in Akobo (as opposed to other places and refugee camps), and so for the time being there really wasn't anything I could aspire to do in order to help or contact her. I imagined her rising with the sun, hearing the cock's crow, and feeling Akobo beginning to hum. During that first year in America, once I was under the covers, I hoped my dreams would carry me back to my beloved mother and Akobo, rather than replay bloodshed and terror—but they rarely did.

Paul and I were butting heads. I was forever grateful that he had played a huge role in getting me to America, but I didn't want him to use that as an excuse to have me under his thumb forever. We ate rice day in and day out, as if we were still receiving food rations from the UN. I let this go, since I didn't have much of an appetite anymore, and instead spent my time riding a bicycle with a Sudanese friend named Gai, who had introduced me to Coke and Sprite, which became my favorite drinks. Once I'd had a taste of soda, I refused to eat at home. I grew thinner and fragile.

I wanted my independence—the freedom America boasted about. And I thought one way to go about gaining it was by earning my own way. So I went to a local Burger King and lied about my age to score a job. I was assigned to work under a short, talkative, energetic African American teenager who spoke so fast I couldn't understand a word he said. My duties included picking up trash from the parking lot and getting supplies from the freezer. I slowly started to learn slang from this kid.

SHAWN: Hey, dawg. Where you from?

ME: Sudan.

SHAWN: Did you see lions there?

ME: Yes.

SHAWN: Did you live with tigers and shit like in the movie *Coming to America*?

ME: No. We had a lot of cows.

I was hoping to save money to send back home to help people with medical bills. However, after two weeks I got fired for always arriving late to work. I didn't understand the concept of punctuality yet. Where I was from, we set our own clocks.

We lived near the YMCA, where there was a basketball court. Both and I would hang out there after school. My height made the African American kids at the court assume that I was good at basketball, and so they always asked me to join their games. This is what sparked my love for basketball. I wanted to assimilate into American culture as quickly as possible, and basketball seemed like a surefire way of doing so.

However, Paul discouraged me from all sports.

PAUL: Only academics will lead to success. Stop this nonsense and come home right after school. You must concentrate on your studies.

But because of my imperfect English, I felt I could excel at physical activities more readily than at academic pursuits. Playing sports was also a great way of making friends—which seemed crucial to surviving American high school—but Paul, with his rigid mindset, refused to recognize that such a thing as play could be important for my future.

But I was not a boy, even if I was not yet a man. I was a hybrid—a boy in age and maybe appearance, but a man in life experience, responsibilities, and, yes, trauma. Basketball gave me a way to express my warrior nature without hurting anyone, and I instinctively understood the importance of channeling my energies in this way. Paul had never been a soldier, so he couldn't comprehend this. I would come back from playing basketball every evening and find Paul at the apartment. Wanting to avoid conflict, I would walk straight to the bedroom Both and I shared, lock myself in there, and cry quietly, thinking about home and my mother.

I was harboring and suppressing a lot of anger, and Both was always underfoot. Paul was on my case, accusing me of leading Both astray, so tensions at home were boiling over. Then one night, as was bound to happen, Both and I had a terrible fight.

ME: I told you not to follow me to the YMCA! You know Paul thinks I'm a "bad influence." You'll get us both in trouble!

BOTH: I don't give a shit about following you around. I'll go where I wanna go and do what I want.

ME: Are you cursing at me?

BOTH: I'm so tired of you complaining, Ger!

Being the older and stronger one, I beat Both up badly, to a point that the neighbors called the police. When they arrived, they reprimanded us and left. After everything cooled off, I left and went to play basketball at the YMCA. I got back and found Paul at home.

PAUL: You are a hopeless child soldier. You refuse to contain your anger. You cannot go on this way. We cannot. You are not walking in the footsteps of the Lord.

My relationship with Paul had deteriorated beyond repair. This, along with his Christian proselytizing, was too much. He had tried micromanaging our so-called family, but Both and I had been soldiers already and had done too much, seen too much, built too much angst and independence to put up with being treated like little children. That fight was the last straw. It was time to flee, to become a wanderer once more.

DISCONNECTED

IN DECEMBER 1994, I GOT in touch with a group of refugees I had known at the Walda and Ifo refugee camps in Kenya. Shortly after I'd come to the United States, they had immigrated to Sioux Falls, South Dakota, some having taken longer routes to America, including through Lebanon. Mostly young adults, they were now living in several apartments in the same building at East Rice Apartments, located right by the main highway. Everyone in the Sudanese refugee community knew that if you wanted a place to hang out and have conversations with fellow countrymen, then South Dakota was the place, and East Rice Apartments was one of the spots.

One of these individuals, James Tot Miak, who was a decade or so older than me, had taken a lot of young refugees under his guardianship. So I approached Paul with a plan in my head.

ME: May I have your permission to visit a group of old friends from Sudan in South Dakota?

PAUL: I think it is a good idea; go during Christmas break.

Once I got to Sioux Falls, I reached out to James Tot Miak using a term of endearment.

ME: Garmiak, I'd like to attend school at Washington High. I was wondering if you could be my guardian while I'm here?

UNCLE JAMES TOT: Did you discuss this with Mr. Paul Ruot?

ME: No, I will call him once I have your answer.

UNCLE JAMES TOT: Well, I am okay with it, Ger. I'll be your guardian if Paul agrees to it.

What I didn't say to either man was that I had been in touch with Thomas Kutey, the boy from the prominent Nairobi family I had befriended when I was at Ifo. He had come to America much earlier than me to seek educational opportunities and was attending high school in Sioux Falls. We had luckily reconnected through the refugee grapevine, and I'd learned he had a driver's license and access to a vehicle almost twenty-four hours a day. This sounded just like the living situation I wanted.

Thomas resided with an older Sudanese refugee, Will,

who had spent many years working in Khartoum, Iraq, Syria, and Lebanon as a military specialist. Will owned the car, which he always left with Thomas. All Thomas had to do was drop Will off at work in the morning, then pick him up in the evening, and, over the weekend, run errands for him, never forgetting to stock his favorite beer. The rest of the time, Thomas and I could drive around, buying chicken and hip-hop radio cassettes whenever we had change left over from Will's errands. Thomas was a fast driver and the music was always loud in the car. The freedom felt good.

It was nice living with other young people in Sioux Falls, including Thomas's younger brother. But there were many Sudanese who, after settling in America, struggled in one way or another. Some had alcohol problems or mental health issues, or couldn't keep a job. We didn't judge them, however. Because of the spirit of brotherhood espoused throughout the community, they always found a place to eat and sleep, no matter how bad things got. This, in a way, allowed them to hide their problems and their shame. The refugee community had its own safety net, guaranteeing them at least the minimum for survival.

Over the break, I started settling into the lifestyle of my refugee friends in South Dakota, spending days and nights talking about old times, joking around, watching American movies, and listening to hip-hop. But because most of us were former child soldiers, we almost always gravitated toward the violent aspects of American pop culture. After seeing gang warfare glorified in films and music videos, we began to fancy ourselves members of either the Bloods or the Crips, and dressed accordingly in their respective gang colors, red and blue.

For the first time in my life, I felt totally liberated, like I was a completely new person. I was finally becoming just a young man in America, my Sudanese past, I thought, vanishing from my psyche. FUBU, Guess, and Karl Kani became the baggy jeans of choice. I wore red bandannas, and within six months, I had picked up English and would now sing along to Scarface and Wu-Tang Clan lyrics.

It had never occurred to me in my wildest imagination that a day would come when I would feel more at home in America and less worried about Sudan and my family. But what I experienced in South Dakota—that sense of disconnection from my past and being transplanted into a present that felt like a distant future—simply blew my mind. I let go of my attachments to the motherland, instead deciding to be American and feel American.

No one knew how to make this happen for me like Thomas Kutey did. And the Sudanese refugee community, which had immersed itself in the gangsta-rap lifestyle of fast cars, nice clothes, and endless partying, created the proper social ecosystem needed for my newfound Americanness to thrive. The lack of a concerned guardian like Paul didn't help matters. My life was now fully in my hands.

THE LOOP

WHEN THE BREAK WAS OVER, I was supposed to go back to Des Moines, back into Paul's custody. But I had become a different person—a much rowdier, more insolent version of myself, which I knew Paul couldn't handle. James Tot Miak had already agreed to enroll me at Washington High School, which my partner in crime, Thomas, attended. James Miak allowed me, like he did all those under his guardianship, to live a somewhat carefree life, where he didn't expect me to go back to his apartment every evening.

At this point, I made my case to Paul that I'd be eighteen in two years, and he agreed I could take care of myself. Frankly, I think he was a little relieved I'd be out of his hair, so that solidified it—I was my own man, on my own.

I spent days hopping from one Sudanese refugee's apartment to another, hanging out with my age-mates. As long as I updated James Tot Miak about my well-being every once in a while, I was scot-free. Everyone in the community knew how liberal, kind, and generous he was, and so no one ever questioned me about why I had such freedom.

Thomas and I were inseparable. We played basketball together and became friends with a cool Ethiopian guy named Girma, who braided his hair and looked like a member of the hip-hop group Bone Thugs-n-Harmony. It was around this time that we discovered something called the Loop, a downtown cruising strip where kids from different high schools brought their parents' cars on weekends. They hung out in parking lots and drove around playing loud music, showing off, and sometimes selling and consuming drugs on the low. Doing the Loop, Thomas told us, was supposed to be a mark of arrival. Whoever stole the show during these sessions became the talk of the town for as long as their fifteen minutes of fame lasted.

The first time we did the Loop, Thomas Kutey took charge, calling me by my nickname (which my friend Musa had given me early on, meaning "symmetrical face" or "lady-like features").

THOMAS: Yo, Nyigeri, this is it! We gotta drive around, play the loudest music with the windows rolled down, and slouch in our seats to show off our brand-new bandannas.

Teenagers of all races, male and female, showed up looking fresh from head to toe, everyone trying to pose like they were the coolest crew. I was a quick learner, and armed with my Thomas- and Girma-sanctioned Americanness, I too acted like I knew what the Loop was all about.

I joined in uttering insults whenever anyone, whether white or black, crossed our crew the wrong way.

THOMAS: Yo, motherfucker, white boy! Pick up the pace, dawg!!!

If members of one race verbally attacked those of another, the rebuttals were instant and unrestricted. Racial superiority was a mirage during the Loop, it seemed, and for the first time in a long while, I occupied a space where one's race didn't mean a thing.

The Loop became a big part of our lives. We hit on white girls, asking them if they wanted to hang out with us. Thomas and Girma made this seem totally normal. To me, it was like a totally alien adventure. But I always went with the flow.

ME: What's up, girl? You wanna talk?

This was the standard pickup line we used whenever we came across a group of girls, and whenever they agreed to hang out with us, we would park our cars next to theirs at the gas station, play some hip-hop, and try to chat them up. The good thing was that none of us were into alcohol at the time, and all that Thomas and I indulged in was basketball and hip-hop. Whatever little money we had went toward sneakers, clothes, and the latest hip-hop releases. That was as far as we went.

But something strange started happening to me after doing the Loop for a long time: I started acting like a roughneck of sorts, and nobody could get through to me, my pent-up fears and anger mounting. Growing up, I had heard stories about my uncle Machiel Duany, who, upon leaving for Khartoum, had cut off all contact with the family, and had never gotten married, which was a big deal in our culture. He only spoke Arabic and was said to have either forgotten how to speak Nuer or simply chosen not to claim it as his language. No one knew what he was up to.

Different stories circulated about my uncle Machiel. Some said he was a mysterious figure in Khartoum, fighting everyone and living a somewhat criminal lifestyle. Everyone was always warned, almost sarcastically, not to follow in Uncle Machiel's footsteps. As I got deeper into the Loop, thoughts of becoming a Machiel kept crossing my mind. I started feeling that, sooner rather than later, I should get a grip on myself before it was too late. But in the meantime, my every action pointed toward my becoming a version of my uncle. I cared less about home and the things that were important to my people. Like a drug, the Loop was my life.

One day, at the basketball court, I had an argument with an African American player, Rob, with whom I'd never enjoyed a cordial relationship. He had referred to me as a "motherfucking African" before, but for the sake of peace, I had ignored his insults. On this particular day, we had rammed into each other during practice, and for some reason, he blamed me for the accidental contact that had left both of us in pain. He stood in front of me, running his mouth, once again calling me a "motherfucking African."

ROB: Are you stupid or something? I will not pass you the rock because you motherfuckas can't handle it with your butterfingers.

ME: Fuck, you too stupid.

ROB: I will beat you and drag you around this basketball court. Say something again, say something, nigga!!!!

I had no issues with being called an African, but at the same time my African pride wouldn't let me allow another man to talk down to me right to my face. I'd had enough of it and pushed him away from me, and that's when all hell broke loose.

In that split second, the raw rage of the warrior in me shot from zero to a hundred. I went at him with blows that he never could've imagined me capable of, beating him up and employing a tactic only a Sudanese boy growing up where I did would: biting him and ripping his skin off with my teeth. Where I came from, biting was a legitimate tactic during a physical fight, but this must have been savagery to the Americans. Bleeding heavily from my bites and in shock that I had done the unimaginable, the guy ran off the court.

ROB: I'ma teach your African behind a lesson!

He was soon out of sight.

ANOTHER PLAYER: That means he's coming back with a gun.

WHITE PLAYER: Thomas, get him off the court! He's not joking. He'll be back with a gun!

Still caught up in my rage, I couldn't leave. Thomas had never seen me fight before, and he too must have been stunned by how his quiet friend had become a completely different creature. An older white man came over and took me by the arm, leading me off the court. He spoke to Thomas.

OLDER WHITE MAN: Hey, please get your friend out of here. For all our sakes.

Thomas got me home but didn't have much to say to me the rest of the night. He did hear some things through the whisper network, though.

THOMAS: Turns out, dude came back with what was probably a gun. He's been looking for you for days. Good thing we ain't go to the same school.

Somehow, this little brush with death didn't stop us from doing the Loop. And our constant presence there put us on the radar of a group of white boys from our school, who seemed to be waiting for the opportunity to initiate a confrontation with us. One evening after school, Thomas, being the fast and cocky driver that he was—what some would call reckless—suddenly overtook the truck belonging to the ringleader of the group of white boys, catching him off guard and causing him to almost swerve.

WHITE DRIVER: Fucking nigger! Who taught you how to drive?

THOMAS: Your mother!

Thomas laughed as we drove off.

WHITE DRIVER: I will see you tomorrow, motherfucker!

The next day, we were back at school, and everything went well until lunch break. Thomas and I had become close friends with two Iraqi brothers, Ahmed and Abdalla, with whom we spoke Arabic. Ahmed and Abdalla were some of the kindest people I had met in my new life in America. Ahmed was a senior, Abdalla was a junior. They had immigrated to America as young kids and become as American as was possible, speaking slang like they were African Americans.

That day, we ate lunch together. As we were leaving the cafeteria, the heavily built and hairy white boy from the previous evening approached us, walking straight at Thomas, and starting with the insults.

WHITE DRIVER: Hey, motherfucker! You were talking trash yesterday. I could fuck you up right now. Who taught you how to drive?

THOMAS: Man, I want no trouble with you.

Thomas kept walking. A group of white boys surrounded us, blocking our way. Before we knew it, the white-boy driver hit Thomas so hard on the back of his head, he almost fell down. Seeing where things were going, I pretended to back off, pulling myself away from the group, as though allowing Thomas to pay for his sins by himself. But as the white boys relaxed, thinking they had Thomas all for themselves, I randomly picked one of them and kicked him so hard in the stomach, he started throwing up. Thomas was yet again surprised at my reckless yet necessary move.

Ahmed and Abdalla joined in, backing Thomas and me up. Before we knew it, the entire cafeteria was in chaos. Seats, food trays, and anything else that could be thrown flew around as more Sudanese and white students joined the fight, each group taking a side without knowing the origin of the brawl. School security quickly rushed in and broke it up. Thomas, a couple of the white boys, and I were given a week's suspension from school. We spent the week hanging around shopping malls.

In May 1995, five months after I arrived in Sioux Falls, I was staying in the East Rice Apartments when James Tot Miak took me aside.

JAMES MIAK: I have received reports from your school that you have been falling asleep in class. I have also spoken with Paul, who assures me you have a good mind and could excel in school if you applied yourself.

The way we're living here is not conducive to your education and overall well-being. I blame myself somewhat for this laissez-faire lifestyle.

ME: Come on, please? I promise to do better.

JAMES MIAK: Even so, I think you should contact your father's brother, Dr. Wal Duany, in Bloomington, Indiana. Ask him if you can live with him and his family and get a decent education, away from me and these terrible influences.

I knew of Uncle Wal Duany, though I had never met him. I'd never thought to contact him before because he was famous in the Sudanese community, a fact that made me feel he was out of my league and reach. He and his wife were both university professors and very active in the Sudanese diaspora. Everybody knew who they were, and there I was, a random son to one of his brother's five wives. Such an important man couldn't be expected to help out every distant relative who contacted him. Nonetheless, Miak took the bold initiative and dialed Uncle Wal's number.

Making what must have been a huge leap of faith and showing an incredible generosity of spirit, Uncle Wal invited me to live with him and his family. I was once again being uprooted from the familiar, being sent to a supposedly better unknown.

Before I left for Uncle Wal's, I ran into my childhood friend Peter Gatkuoth. He had made the trek to Walda not long after I left Akobo. Being nineteen at the time, he had managed to travel to America on his own.

PETER: You've got a new life and new experiences, indeed. I am so excited that you speak perfect English.

ME: And I am excited to see you, Peter. What's the word?

PETER: Did I ever tell you what really happened to that journalist Simon's camera?

ME: What do you mean? That soldier took it. Whatever happened to him? Did he die in the battle at Baliet?

PETER: No one knows his fate for sure, Ger. Except that all Nube soldiers drowned in the Nile. So if man didn't get him, nature surely did. But I know mine and Airborne's fate for sure. . . . It was us, Ger. Airborne Boy and I took the camera and lenses because we wanted them. We hid the equipment in the bush. We didn't even know how to use it; we just were annoyed that Simon had it.

ME: And you never told anyone.

PETER: Only his girlfriend, Nyankor. And now there's only me who even could. Maybe it was karma. It left Airborne Boy and Nyankor dead and me alive, suffering inside, unable to unburden myself, with their deaths and that of the soldier crushing my conscience. Eating me alive.

ME: Why didn't you tell me?

PETER: You always had a big mouth. What would you have done?

ME: You're right. Probably told. Peter Gatkuoth, we all did bad things, sometimes on purpose, sometimes not. What matters is that every day into the future, we do better.

PETER: You are right. Our generation has been devastated by events no human should ever have to face. We didn't know better. Life in Akobo remains ugly!

ME: It was our turn to fight the battles, but those who are in a position to kill today will be killed tomorrow. This is a vicious cycle.

PETER: Nigeeri, you were always a gifted kid with some sense. Look at you now, so mature. Maybe one day things will be normal again. And maybe one day we will recognize what normal is. Nothing is impossible, brother.

I sensed something was a little off with Peter. He didn't care much for school, preferring to chase the freedom that America offered—both a blessing and a curse. But now that I knew he was here, it helped me feel like I was not alone. We said good-bye, and once again I dove into the unfamiliar. I wondered what would happen to my friends who continued living an amped-up version of the thug life we'd led in refugee camps. I too felt the strong pull of that life, as it was familiar, but I was off on yet another journey, given yet another opportunity to make something of myself. I hoped I deserved it.

A NEW FAMILY

AFTER A LONG BUS RIDE, I hopped in a cab, which took me to the Tulip Tree Apartments in Bloomington, Indiana. They called my uncle down to settle the cab fare, but instead of doing so, he got into a verbal altercation with the driver.

> UNCLE WAL: What do you mean, a hundred dollars? You are trying to take advantage. You should have told him to take the train, which would've been much cheaper. I will pay you sixty dollars and that's it!

The moment I walked through the door into the spacious three-bedroom apartment, I felt a sense of redemption. I was being given a chance to start life over with my uncle and his wife, both doctorate degree holders, and their sons Bil and Kueth and daughters, Nyagon and Nok. Their eldest son, my cousin Duany, was away at the University of Wisconsin. So much smarts in one place.

UNCLE WAL: Everyone, please meet Ger. He's the cousin from Sudan about whom I've been telling you guys.

AUNTIE JULIA: Let me show you to your room.

ME: Yes, Auntie Julia.

AUNTIE JULIA: You will be sharing it with your cousins Bil and Kueth. But please feel welcome. That's the shower over there. You can have a quick one before dinner is served.

My cousins came to me with warm smiles and outstretched arms, the Sudanese way, giving me a long group embrace that made me feel like we had known each other all along. I hadn't felt such love and warmth for a long time.

Kueth was away at basketball practice and came back just after I'd had a shower and changed my clothes. I heard someone opening the bedroom door and saw a tall, dark young man about my age walking in. He could have passed for one of my Sudanese friends I'd grown up with, were it not for his heavy American accent.

KUETH: Hey, Dad. This is Ger?

UNCLE WAL: Yes, that's your cousin.

KUETH: He looks more like Duany.

Kueth's brother Duany was a basketball legend, so I took that as a compliment. I stood up and went to greet him the Sudanese way, by patting him on both shoulders before embracing him, but Kueth had no idea what I was up to. He stood there beaming.

KUETH: Hey, Ger, how are you doing, man? It's really great to finally meet you. Dad's been talking about you a lot. How was your journey here?

ME: I'm doing great, Kueth. It's really nice to meet you too. The trip was eventful but nothing unusual.

I don't know why I couldn't speak the truth about my journey and the atrocities I'd witnessed or the trials I'd faced. Maybe I thought it just wasn't the right time. Maybe I thought there'd never be a right time to relive all that.

KUETH: I'm glad that you made it. This is home. I think you'll like it here. If there's anything I can do for you, please don't hesitate to let me know.

From our first meeting, I knew my cousin Kueth and I would have a special friendship. He seemed genuine and unpretentious, and we bonded over our love of basketball. My uncle did more formal introductions at the dinner table later that evening, telling my cousins part of my story and saying that his first priority was to get me an education.

UNCLE WAL: Ger is your brother. We all have to find ways of supporting him so he can get a proper education and make something of himself.

One of the first things I noticed in my uncle's household was that everyone had a right to speak and share their opinion at the dinner table, including Bil, the youngest in the family. It was completely opposite to life in Sudan, where my father's word was law. I was now part of a world that was not restricted by the culture and traditions from back home. I found it difficult to fit in at first, accustomed to the carefree life on the streets of Sioux Falls. My first obstacle was language. My cousins, uncle, and auntie spoke proper English, while mine was heavily littered with street slang. I had to check myself every time I spoke to make sure I didn't use any expletives, which was the norm in my previous life.

I spent the summer with Kueth, working on a few people's lawns during our spare time, and made some pocket change while developing a work ethic, which my uncle insisted I do. Then, during dinner one evening, he brought up my returning to Sioux Falls and the topic of my education.

UNCLE WAL: Getting an education is what Ger needs most at this point in his life. I think he should head back to South Dakota before the school year starts up again.

I think he felt his family was big enough and also knew I had a reputation for fighting. Everyone seemed to think it wasn't a good idea, however. My cousin Duany, who was home from the University of Wisconsin, piped up first.

DUANY: Dad, look at Ger. He has the physique to play basketball. Let him stay and have Kueth teach him how to play better. He can take my spot in the bedroom while I'm away at school.

With all my cousins rooting for me to stay, my uncle was outnumbered.

UNCLE WAL: Ger, if you are to start school here, I have a little test for you. I want you to write a composition. Your auntie and I will look at it, then decide if you can be a sophomore.

I was a little older than Kueth, but due to my late schooling, I would now be a sophomore with him—if everything went according to plan. I did my level best.

To my uncle and Aunt Julia,
    I am writing this letter to beg you that I like to stay here in Bloomington Indiana. It is good chance to get your guidance in this strange land.

I will be a good family members in this house. I left Sudan because there was no school but my mother and father did not believe that I could be here with you in the USA. I will complete my education, with hope that I will return to serve our family in Dengjock Village.

In Itang camp, my level of education is primary school but when I arrive in Ifo camp in 1993, we did not get any schooling. I know how to write in Nuer language. I know how to speak Arabic very well. If I can spend time here in Bloomington, I believe I can succeed as a junior in high school instead of sophomore. I am so embarrassed to attend classes with children in which are two to three years younger then I am.

I held my breath as I handed it to my aunt.

AUNTIE JULIA: Hey, Ger, you sure have good handwriting.

Auntie passed the paper around the house for everyone to see. At that point in time, I knew I couldn't express myself that well in prose, but the one thing I had going for me was exceptional handwriting. The upside to having to sit and write this composition was that I was allowed to stay with this new crop of relatives and start school!

As low as my grades were, my uncle took me to school and insisted I be made a sophomore. I had other ideas.

ME: Uncle, why not let me be a junior in high school?

UNCLE WAL: Ger, things don't work like that here. Let me tell you *my* story. When colonizers had control over Sudan, they cultivated an education system based on the white man's knowledge and culture. They actually asked chiefs of our villages to give up their children to go to school. But my father, Duany, refused to give us kids up while your father, Thabach, was still young. Later, he did allow me and the Honorable Peter Gual Kuiny to attend their schools. I arrived in America in the sixties, with tribal marks across my forehead, and was sent to school as an older child. And due to this educational opportunity, the Honorable Peter Gual became the leader of South Sudan. And I served as minister of finance in South Sudan until Sharia law was introduced. It doesn't matter how old you are, education is lifelong learning. Even if I had been forty years old, I would have had to start at the beginning, until I reached higher learning.

It was important to me not to be socially behind my peers, even if academically I needed extra help. I thought it would help my emotional growth and self-esteem. Concepts and mathematical laws will come to you in time, whereas shame can leave you back decades. But I lost my argument with my uncle, so sophomore it was.

I knew I could play basketball, run track, and play

soccer, and said as much during the admission process. I scored four goals in my first soccer scrimmage, making me an instant star on the field. But when I went to the basketball court, the first thing the coach told me was that I was too skinny.

COACH MCKINNEY: Hey! Young man! You've got to eat. You've got to build some muscle.

I eat to survive, I said to myself. I wondered if any American could understand that.

SUFFERING IN SILENCE

AMERICANS DIDN'T GET ME. I didn't get them. I became a complete recluse, never talking unless I had to. I retreated and only observed, taking in whatever I needed to. And the only person that could see through the facade was Kueth. No one understood me better than my cousin, so I confided in him.

KUETH: Do you still speak Nuer or Arabic?

ME: Yes, Arabic is the common language that unites the northern and southern Sudanese. But our real language is Thok Naath.

KUETH: I used to speak Arabic because we were born in Juba. We have all forgotten Arabic and Nuer.

ME: I can teach you how to speak Nuer very well.

KUETH: Do you know how to write Thok Naath?

ME: Yes, I'm actually a good teacher in Thok Naath. And swimming is my thing too. I can teach you how.

KVETH: Tell me something about the Nile.

ME: When I was in Sudan, my friends and I went to play in the Nile. We were jumping from fifteen feet above the river because the river was deep during that season. One afternoon, a good friend named Jimmy dove in, not knowing some evil people had stuck their spears, straight up, deep under the surface. Jimmy was impaled to death.

It was an example of what I'd witnessed in my everyday life. Just one trauma among countless others.

We spoke late into the night about my childhood back in Sudan, the wars, the famine, and the long treks. Those were the nights when I couldn't sleep and tossed and turned like soiled clothes in the washer, haunted and drained by memories of things at once so distant in the past in Sudan yet also lurking, stealthily in my mind, ready to ambush my spirit at any time.

Throughout high school, basketball was the only thing that helped me escape the tortured thoughts and festering anger that soldiering and other childhood traumas had drilled deep into my psyche.

I studied English during the day, and spent the bulk of my free time practicing my dribble and jump shots. I remembered a blue-eyed lawyer in Ifo, with his starched white shirt and pressed khaki trousers, who told me how I would be good at basketball. His prediction was right. My lanky frame served me well, as I had speed and agility.

I had ended my partying and gang posturing—I no longer stayed up late watching violent movies or wore gang-affiliated clothing. And instead, for the first time, I excelled at school and basketball. The game brought me praise, the team made me feel like a member of a supportive community, and following Coach McKinney's instructions taught me to focus. For some reason, I was better able to follow the rules of my basketball coach than those of any other adult I'd met thus far in America. I'd found a way to communicate, to release my pent-up aggression, and to follow a leader I respected, who seemed to actually care about my well-being.

However, whenever I tried talking about my life in Africa, people thought I was joking or even lying. They couldn't comprehend the world I described, partly because I had trouble putting my experiences into words. This was especially true of my new family, my cousins in particular, who barely remembered Sudan. If I'd been in their shoes, I'm sure I too would have found the events I described not only inhumane but also far-fetched. My delivery was an issue as well, because I didn't seem horrified or even sad when I disappeared inside my head to draw out these memories—those everyday realities of normal life in Sudan. Other times, I thought recounting these things would scare my cousins, so I made a conscious decision to keep most of my past bottled up. I was an expressive person by nature, which made this emotionally difficult, and I forced myself to turn inward. Instead of dealing with my sadness, frustrations, and fear, I chose to study hard so that one day I'd have the tools to tell my story without any inhibitions, and the opportunity to rescue and recover my whole self once again.

During my senior year, in 1998, my team, the Cougars, played our rival, Martinsville. Our opponents, a white team made up essentially of people from the Indiana Klan, had a reputation for being racist, and our coach prepared us for this. The funny thing was, having been where I'd been, and seen what I'd seen, and done what I'd done, the last thing anyone could use to hurt me now was words. There was no verbal insult that could damage my confidence. The wind just blew it away.

COACH MCKINNEY: Do not let Martinsville get under your skin. They're notorious for acting up and shouting racist things to throw you off your game. Don't take the bait. Just win. That'll hurt them most.

When the game began, a Martinsville player aggressively targeted Kueth. It got to the point where he punched Kueth in the groin.

MARTINSVILLE PLAYER: You fucking nigger.

The referee brushed off the incident.

KUETH: Ref! He punched me! He's a racist too!

REF: Double technical foul on the Cougars.

COACH MCKINNEY: Kueth! Keep your cool or you'll lose the game for us! I don't care if it's fair or not!

And as so often happens when no one stands on principle, another Martinsville player later felt emboldened enough to hit Kueth in the stomach, which caused him to vomit on the floor.

Aunt Julia screamed from the crowd in Nuer as I dashed to Kueth's side, and the entire gym erupted, with opposing crowds shouting at each other. The chaos and rage transported me back to the front lines of war, and I felt the urge to kill rise up inside me. Before I could do anything I would regret, the officials called off the game. Police escorted our enraged team onto the buses. ESPN covered the incident the following day. In a strange way, this horrible episode helped me come closer to understanding that there were memories and emotions deep within me—like land mines strewn about my brain—that could easily be triggered.

I woke up in the middle of the night, seized with terror, dreaming that I was back on the hot battlefield, my gun jamming. I felt alone in my anguished mind and didn't think there was anyone who'd understand my horror.

MY THEORY OF RELATIVITY

I GRADUATED FROM HIGH SCHOOL in 1998 at the age of twenty and felt that I could achieve anything I set my mind to—as long as I kept my warrior's temper under control. I accepted a basketball scholarship to Lake Land College, a community college in Mattoon, Illinois. Despite the odds stacked against me, I was well on my way toward fulfilling that abstract dream Oder had once had for me—getting educated. I wonder if he'd even conceived of me getting a higher education. I surely hadn't.

My uncle and cousin Kueth dropped me off at school.

UNCLE WAL: Ger, this is a new beginning where you can redefine yourself. Know that athletic scholarships have no meaning without world-class performance. Keep working hard in school so that you can get into a four-year college.

KUETH: Hey, G-man. Please go bust their guys so that you can get a full scholarship to Division I!

UNCLE WAL: Here's twenty dollars to buy yourself lunch.

ME: Thank you, Dad. I will be in touch!

Kueth would be off to Syracuse University the following day.

Within the first week, I met a woman named Carla, a white lady from Mattoon, who became my tutor, mentor, and friend all rolled into one. Everyone else on the basketball team seemed to have a grip on their grades, but since I hadn't had a solid academic foundation, Carla became the person who filled that gap for me. I'd say she was at least forty years old, but we bonded on a deeper level because I had lived a life well beyond my young years. As she helped me with my studies, Carla and I became close, to a point where I started confiding in her about my past. I felt comfortable and safe. I felt heard and not judged. I felt believed. Carla was a good listener, never one to draw premature conclusions. She seemed to really care about me and what I had to tell her, which gave me the confidence to open up to her more. One day she asked me a simple, straightforward question.

CARLA: Where is your family, Ger?

She didn't press the issue. She allowed me to tell her more, bit by bit, and say only what I felt comfortable expressing at any given time.

ME: Maybe in Sudan.

That one question of hers compelled me to open the floodgates. I surprised myself with how much I was saying. I felt that weights were being lifted from my chest and heart, that I could breathe easier each day and night, and that speaking about the ghosts of my past released them into the ether, such that they would no longer haunt me and I would not have to carry them with me anymore.

As much as Carla's kindness helped me heal, a lot of that positivity was undone by the Lake Land College coach, Coach Dudley. I had sometimes had trouble getting access to my Pell Grant money, and wondered if he had my best interests at heart. Luckily, that summer I was selected as part of a group of up-and-coming college basketball players to participate in the junior college games at Indiana State University, where coaches from across the country came to scout for young talent. At the championships, I got spotted by Coach Mack of Los Angeles Southwest College, who was impressed by my speed and shooting skills. He approached me when I was gathering my belongings from the bleachers after my game.

COACH MACK: Yo! What's happening?

ME: I was trying to put the clamp on 'em boys!

COACH MACK: Where you from?

ME: Bloomington, Indiana.

COACH MACK: No. Originally?

ME: I am from Sudan.

COACH MACK: Oh, snap! You know Duany Duany?

ME: Yes, he is my blood brother. We are both from Sudan by way of Bloomington.

COACH MACK: You got a nice fadeaway like Duany Duany, and I like that you can hops outta too. Bro, we gotta get you in a weight room because you are light in the ass! But you can shoot the rock like Lamar Odom, and are quick on your feet like KB. Here's my number. I want you to come to Southern California to make a name for yourself.

ME: Word?

COACH MACK: Yes, I have a few players from Chi-Town, because Chicago's my hometown. LA is a beautiful place. You can play ball all year round.

We bonded over being Midwesterners, and he invited me to Los Angeles with a promise of a full scholarship.

COACH MACK: You never know who you'll meet in Los Angeles. It's the one place your life can take a huge turn for the better at any point in time.

His offer appealed to me, but the distance from Indiana to Los Angeles made me hesitant. I'd been moving my whole life. I wanted to stick somewhere, fit in, plant roots, nourish myself, sprout and flourish.

At the end of that summer, I went back to my uncle's in Bloomington, where I shared the scholarship news. My aunt seemed very displeased with what appeared to be my recklessness in considering a move to Los Angeles.

AUNTIE JULIA: Ger, what are you doing?

ME: I think it would be good for me. I can play basketball, get a great education, and save even more with this scholarship.

AUNTIE JULIA: Your stepbrother Ruot went to Los Angeles in 1989. Do you know what happened to him?

ME: Yes . . .

AUNTIE JULIA: He was drugged and robbed. Do you want the same thing to happen to you?

Ruot was my stepmother Elizabeth's son, whom my uncle had brought to America in the 1980s. That ugly incident was the go-to story one told whenever Los Angeles came up. But since I longed to escape Coach Dudley's sphere of influence, I made the decision to go to Los Angeles, despite resistance from the family. Meanwhile, some of my Sudanese friends from the refugee camps were now living in Michigan. So I hopped on a Greyhound bus to check on them before continuing on to the City of Angels. I located my childhood friend Lual Nyang, the proper English speaker who had owned the soccer ball and given his only pair of jeans to me when I came to America. Lual had managed to emigrate from the refugee camp in Kenya a little after me. He was in his third year at the University of Michigan in Ann Arbor, studying nursing.

The day I arrived, Lual and I stayed up through the night talking about our journeys. He looked very fit and healthy, so the nickname Scrawny Boy no longer fit him. In the days that followed, we'd spend our free time working out, and marveling at how as kids we ate to survive, yet now we ate to stay healthy. I also couldn't thank him enough for those jeans—how, even though they were a gift for America, because he'd given them to me, they reminded me of home.

Eventually, he admitted there was something he needed to get off his chest.

LUAL: I'm not sure how to say this, Ger. But . . . you and I, we are cousins. And I'm sorry I kept that from you.

ME: Are you joking? How could we be related?

LUAL: I never wanted you to find out about this because I didn't want you to think of me as your enemy.

ME: You are not my enemy. We are great friends. Forever.

LUAL: The marriage that binds us was controversial. It united two enemy Nuer ethnic groups. Your side fought for the SPLA, and mine for Anya Anya II. I kept this secret our whole lives.

ME: This is big news, Lual. And, yes, I am surprised. But nothing could ever come between us.

First, Oder revealed he was my half brother; now Lual was telling me he and I were actually related. This revelation gave me one of my own: the people I love are my family, whether we're related or not.

One day, I received a call from Paul, my former benefactor.

PAUL: Ger, I am flying back to Sudan to visit my parents. I will be in Akobo. Your mother might still be there. . . .

I wrote a letter for him to give to her and tucked my high school graduation photo, a photo of me playing basketball, and two hundred dollars inside the envelope. I felt immense relief at the notion that, finally, I could reassure my mother that I was alive. I addressed her using her Christian name.

> *Dear Mary Nyathak,*
> *I hope this letter reaches you in peace and in the name of our almighty God. I've reached America, Mother. I am a bigger boy. I also*

graduated from high school last year. My only trouble in this strange land is that I miss you, and in all these years I haven't been able to stop thinking about you, Nyakuar, Both, and Gok. I sometime wonder if you are still in good health, because I heard there's been killing between the Lou Nuer and Jikany Nuer over water and livestock.

If you get this letter, I would love to simply hear all your voices and speak with you over the telephone during the dry season.

I am hoping that you'll keep this $200 for your transportation to the Gambella region. If you can buy food, it would be good for my brothers and sister Nyakuar. And please pass my greetings on to Uncle Reat Muon, and tell him that I didn't forget to come back home.

Sincerely,
Gabriel Ger Thabach Duany

BALL'S IN MY COURT

THE BUS RIDE TO LOS ANGELES was long and tiresome. African American passengers on the bus started singing at some point, trying to make the journey less boring. Almost everyone was on their way to a new life in a new city. I arrived midmorning and headed for a pay phone to call Coach Mack, which had been my instructions. I tried him a couple of times, but no one was picking up. In time, all the other passengers found their rides and departed, leaving me stranded and alone in a foreign place. Had I not already been through war, famine, and everything in between, I might have been scared. Instead, I just waited for an hour or two and tried again. This time he picked up and made his way to the bus station.

COACH MACK: Hey, Ger, welcome to the City of Angels!

He drove me to a house owned by a lady named Tracie, an extremely beautiful and hospitable mother of three, who was housing other basketball players brought in by Coach Mack, who was an assistant to the head coach, Reggie Morris. Not long after, I got recruited to join Los Angeles Southwest College, an offer that came with a full scholarship. Even though Coach Mack had gotten me out here, nothing was a given. I had to earn my place on the team—and then keep it. I became the token African guy who plays hard on the basketball court, and all of a sudden everyone in the neighborhood wanted a piece of me.

TYPICAL NEIGHBOR: So how was it growing up in Africa?

They didn't care—not really. But I'd engage in small talk, never divulging enough about my experience to let them in, but not putting them off by acting indifferent either.

One evening, I was scrimmaging with a few teammates. I was training hard and trying to focus more on my physical fitness so I could blow away the competition when it was game time.

My opponent on offense was charging upcourt with the ball, and I used some smooth moves to shut him down. I cut him off, forcing him to give up the ball, which clearly rankled him. He threw his body weight at me such that I fell and bent my thumb back. I was rushed to the university health services to have it looked at, and then braced in a splint.

My heart broke when I got the news: I'd torn a ligament in my thumb, which meant staying off the court for a good chunk of the remainder of the season and most likely not getting my scholarship renewed. I'd be unable to afford to return next semester.

As I ran out the clock on my college career, one afternoon I sat down behind the theater building on campus, passing time before my computer information systems class. Out of nowhere, an African American gentleman with a square forehead and teeth like a goat's approached me.

GENTLEMAN: Hey, how are you? Do you come from Africa?

ME: Yes, I come from Sudan in Africa.

GENTLEMAN: I work in the theater arts department as the acting coach, and we're producing an Africa-themed play. Why don't you drop by the rehearsals and see if it's something that would interest you?

ME: Sure. I wouldn't mind checking it out.

The invitation to the rehearsal came as a timely, much-needed break. I was studying hard and spent a lot of time alone, sometimes passing by the gym to watch my former teammates train. I'd catch myself lost in thought about my predicament now that I was injured. If basketball didn't work out, could I craft a professional career for myself, or would I spiral downward and become a loser?

I went to the rehearsal the following day just to see what it was like to act in the theater. I watched the actors discussing their characters and working on their African accents. The play was about kings, queens, and warriors, and how their strong cultures have sustained the continent. More specifically, it centered on Jaja of Opobo, king of a Nigerian city-state who, much like America's Frederick Douglass, was known for his political acumen and stunning intellect and for having freed himself from slavery.

The director-playwright was a curvaceous African American lady with big brown eyes. She always dressed in black pants with a black shirt and seemed so sophisticated and erudite. She wore her hair in Afro puffs similar to those of the rapper the Lady of Rage.

After the play, she took me backstage.

DIRECTOR: Hey, guys, we have a new warrior, Ger.

ME: Hello, guys.

ACTORS: Welcome to our family.

DIRECTOR: We've finally got an actor who can fit the role of an African warrior. He's from Sudan. Isn't he handsome? How many languages do you speak?

ME: About four.

DIRECTOR: I'd like for you to say something in your language, if you are comfortable, but no pressure.

Your presence alone with your spear in your hand will be great.

I found it a little hilarious, to be asked to stand bare-chested, holding a spear. It reminded me of home in Sudan. Easy enough, I figured.

What excited me most was the ability to be part of the cast, to watch in silence as people recited their lines onstage. We rehearsed three times a week, and my job was to stand there like a statue. There was always an audience watching the rehearsals, and they all got the sense that maybe I couldn't speak proper English and thus had been given the role of a human prop, never to say a word. But when they'd hear me speak after rehearsals, they'd then wonder why I wasn't being given a single line to recite. But I was the one holding me back, not anyone involved in the production. I still hadn't figured out how best to express myself in America.

And then one day during rehearsals, I took a leap of faith.

At one point in the play, instead of standing in place, as instructed, I jumped down from the stage with no shirt on and the spear in my hand and roared.

ME: *Hululululu!*

I'd felt the moment in my bones. I knew that my action was honest—it's what a man in that position, a man guarding his king, would have done. Everyone in the theater was shocked: my character had never done that before. The other actors went silent. The rehearsal audience clapped and roared.

AUDIENCE: Yeah!

Later on, as we debriefed backstage, the playwright singled me out. She was thrilled by the excitement my improvisation had generated.

PLAYWRIGHT: Ger, that was a powerful move you did out there!

ME: Thank you.

ACTING COACH: I think it's high time we got you some lines. You're not shy, you just needed to feel the truth of the moment in your gut. You needed to find your voice.

The play ran for a number of days, to a full house each time. Word had gone out that I'd joined the play's cast, and everyone who knew me from the basketball court showed up just to see me in action. The acting coach, the gentleman who had first approached me to join the play, told me I should consider taking acting more seriously, pointing out that well-honed acting skills could land me in places and spaces I hadn't imagined inhabiting, especially in Los Angeles.

ACTING COACH: The truth is, you can do more in LA with acting.

ME: You think so? I am just a basketball player. I don't think I can last long in this business.

ACTING COACH: We will help you train, brother!

Although at that time it seemed like mere talk, I enrolled in some theater classes to gain credits toward graduation. I realized I enjoyed acting as an outlet for my own emotions. I could embody the life experiences of another person, channel their inner selves, express their joy, pain, anger, or suffering—and release my own in the process. It was a kind of catharsis—a better release than any of the others I'd tried so far (fighting, partying, retreating, hiding). And it was a way to bridge my past and the future.

A LOST BOY

MY THUMB HEALED NOT LONG after my theatrical debut, and so I returned to the basketball court, where my team was headed to the state finals.

My first game back after my injury, Coach Reggie played a 2-3 zone defense, where I was a wingman. I anticipated a pass from my opponent, found myself on a fast break being chased down by defense, and dribbled the ball to the hoop, jamming it down the net's throat off one foot like Dr. J from the 1970s. But I landed wrong and my knee popped. Loud. I'd never experienced such pain in my life. I was holding my knee, but the referee ignored it until Coach Reggie called a time-out. A couple of my teammates came over and carried me off the court.

A hospital scan revealed the degree of my injury: a torn ACL. My team had won, and everyone, especially Coach Reggie, was in a jovial mood, but I was ambivalent. Because of the recovery time needed to heal my injury, I knew I was going to lose my scholarship.

Take three: After a few months to regroup, I tried out for and won a basketball scholarship to the University of Bridgeport in Connecticut to play in Division II. Although I hadn't yet played Division I, this seemed like a demotion, but it was better than not playing at all.

My first day at Bridgeport, I attended a psychology class taught by a tall, passionate, youthful professor named Dr. Pedro. He captured everyone's attention whenever he spoke, and opened my eyes to a new kind of calling: working with and helping others.

He explained that child psychology was the most important subject to learn since that's where all our traumas begin, and that children develop differently from adults. Once you are able to understand your own childhood psychology, you can then learn how to explain, predict, and control your adult self.

I switched my major from computer information systems to human services. Immediately afterward, as he'd done with all his students, Dr. Pedro asked me about my early life. I told him about my time as a soldier.

DR. PEDRO: Do you ever have nightmares or violent thoughts?

ME: Of course I do.

DR. PEDRO: There's something called post-traumatic stress disorder. Ever heard of it?

ME: No.

DR. PEDRO: It's something you and I should look into and talk about. Sound good?

ME: Okay. Sure.

DR. PEDRO: I suggest you take a look at *Man's Search for Meaning*, by Viktor Frankl, which, in a way, changed my life. I began to change my outlook on life and confront myself and my issues openly, in pursuit of peace from within.

Dr. Pedro became to me at the University of Bridgeport what Carla was to me at Lake Land College—a teacher, mentor, and confidant. He and I had long talks after lectures, and he helped me understand why, for so many years, I had experienced violent flashbacks and night terrors.

DR. PEDRO: Refugees, yourself included, often don't find the help they need in dealing with their demons.

ME: If they can't understand the past, how can they build a future in their new homelands?

DR. PEDRO: Exactly. And keeping your thoughts to yourself keeps you in a mental prison. It's time we got you out.

On the court, Coach Mike had a laid-back approach to basketball, which I was not accustomed to. Training had always felt like military camp, where the coach was the general and we players his battalion. That was my comfort zone—it's what I understood, where my upbringing came in handy. Playing at Bridgeport wasn't as demanding as I wanted it to be, but I stayed on since I needed the scholarship. Meanwhile, I joined my cousin Kueth at Syracuse University during breaks, where a group of us worked on building an international basketball career.

There was a huge portrait in the gym of my famed countryman and former NBA star Manute Bol. Manute stood at an unimaginable seven feet seven, the tallest man I had ever seen. He cared deeply about Sudanese refugees and liked to hold gatherings of Sudanese athletes at his house in Connecticut. One day he had me, my cousin Kueth, the future NBA star Luol Deng and his brother Ajou Deng, a fine player called Deng Gai, and many others over, where we formed a team called the Lost Boys, after the term for the children of Sudan who were orphaned or whose lives were uprooted by war. (The Red Cross had come to our Ifo refugee camp and found a group of us living together in one tent, without mothers or fathers around. Each time they asked where our parents were, one of us would randomly, lightly state we were boys without mothers. So the aid workers branded us the "Lost Boys of Sudan" or "Red Soldiers," meaning child soldiers.)

We played different teams and raised money for causes back in Sudan. And Manute played alongside us. His friends Mark and Shannon Murphy, Andrew Kearns, and Eddie Bono were always present, part of the charity efforts. One day Manute gathered us all together at the Murphys'. I was seated on the porch, close to the hoop, indulging in some hot dogs and barbecued chicken. I got a knot in my stomach, fearing this part of my basketball career was about to come to a screeching halt due to some random injury. In a way it was, but not for the reason I expected.

MANUTE: I have received a call from a woman named Jane Fonda and her adopted daughter, Mary Williams. They are in Atlanta looking for Lost Boys.

ME: The Lost Boys of Sudan? Us?

MANUTE: Yes, in fact. Those of us displaced by war and torn away from our families. They want real Lost Boys to audition for a part in a Hollywood film.

ME: Is this for real? What movie?

MANUTE: *I Heart Huckabees.*

Manute gave us instructions on how to shoot an audition video, encouraging each of us to give it a try. Our host, Mark, together with Andrew Kearns, who was an attorney, took charge of the auditions in Mark's living room.

While waiting our turn, we played ball. After about thirty minutes, I went inside and stood in front of the camera. I felt that slight twinge of nerves that bubbles up in your belly and makes you want to either throw up or shake and warm your whole body, like before a basketball game. Luckily, my short stint hanging around the theater arts crew at Los Angeles Southwest College helped me channel those emotions into my performance.

We did the dinner table scene. Mark read the lines with me. When it was my turn to speak, my heart beat faster than when I tore down the court for a layup. I blurted out my line.

ME: "Because it is a family tradition in which I should continue."

ANDREW: Cut!

It was exhilarating and heady, and then it was over. Unlike in the theater, there was no applause from the crowd. No curtain call. No flowers for the star on opening night. But that's okay. This might have been a different animal, but I loved it just as much. Somehow, being someone else for even a moment made me feel as though I understood myself a little bit better. I took everything I'd been through, everything I'd learned, and focused it on creating something positive. It felt right.

FIRST-CLASS TREATMENT

PAUL JANGJUOL, THE MINISTER WHO had ushered us out of Sudan and with whom I'd lived in Des Moines, finally returned to America, bringing along another set of refugees with him, and news that my mother was alive and well.

ME: Paul, welcome back! How's my mum and the boys? And Nyakuar?

PAUL: She wept with joy when I gave her your letter.

I felt ecstatic, knowing my mother was aware I was still alive. But that was displaced by an immediate silence between us. Soon I was holding my breath as though I'd sunk beneath the waves of the Nile, waiting for Paul to say whatever it was he clearly didn't want to.

PAUL: Ger. It's your elder brother Chuol.

I knew it. It was as though good news could never travel without its older, wiser chaperone: bad.

PAUL: He tried to follow the same path as you to the States but somehow got waylaid in Addis Ababa. He ended up living on the streets there, alone and lonely and . . .

ME: He died?

PAUL: From either starvation or disease.

ME: Like so many other Lost Boys.

We are the Lost Boys of Sudan—lost because, in fleeing war, we scattered across the earth. Lost because, once we stopped running, we struggled to find a purpose. Lost because, wherever we settled, no one knew what to do with us. Lost because, no matter where we went, we didn't know what to do with ourselves.

My brother was victim of a madness brought on by what I could now identify as post-traumatic stress disorder. Without ever being physically wounded, he was yet another casualty of war. Historians and politicians go on and on about those who died, who lost their lives in war—but not those who lived, whose lives were lost like mine. And Chuol's. Survivors—but now ghosts of who we once were.

I was devastated, haunted by this news, but I simply couldn't allow myself to think about it. If I did, sorrow and survivor's guilt would have sent me plummeting into a heavy depression. Despite my decision to move forward, I caught myself crying quietly at night, reenacting Chuol's predicament in my mind. I quietly mourned my brother and refused to share the news with anyone, pushing my pain deeper and deeper inside my organs. Locking it up tight.

I tried hard not to fall back into old self-destructive habits and got back to basketball and school. At some point, while visiting Kueth at Syracuse, I was taking a nap in his dorm room after a workout when the phone rang.

KUETH: Hello? . . . Ger! Telephone!

ME: Who would be calling me here?

KUETH: How should I know?

I picked up the receiver.

ME: Hello?

VOICE: Ger?

ME: Yes. That's me.

VOICE: My name is Mary Vernieu. I'm one of the casting directors for the film *I Heart Huckabees*. We'd like to offer you a role in our upcoming movie at Universal Studios.

ME : Really? That's very nice. Thank you.

I hung up the phone. Kueth knew exactly what had happened and went ballistic.

KUETH: Ger, my man, I told you! I told you they'd pick you, my man!

I didn't understand the magnitude of the news. It could have been that Chuol's death was eating me up silently, tamping down any emotion I might otherwise have felt. I was just . . . neutral—about everything—though my insides were tearing themselves apart. Manute and Shannon called shortly after.

MANUTE : Ger, man, you've got the role. Everyone here is ecstatic!

Not too long after, I received in the mail a yellow draft of the script. Every night, Kueth and I stayed up and went through it, trying to get me into the proper state of mind for playing the part. Kueth's enthusiasm never subsided one bit.

KUETH: Ger, man, you'll be the Will Smith of Sudan, man!

A few weeks later, I received an airline ticket to Los Angeles from Universal Studios. I was to spend three weeks shooting, playing a character named Stephen Nimieri.

For the first time in my life, I flew first class. And that's when I began sensing something huge was happening. This was unlike my trip across the Atlantic.

I was seated next to well-dressed men and women, and the basketball player in me, wearing shorts and a white T-shirt, felt a lot out of place. The seats were made of leather and I had room to stretch out my long legs. I was offered champagne, but I wasn't much of a drinker, so I buried myself in the script instead. I could hardly concentrate, though, my mind wandering to thoughts of how I got here and why me.

I landed in Los Angeles and was met by a chauffeur holding a placard with my name on it. He opened the back door of a black limousine for me and drove me to my hotel, the Marina del Rey, a side of the city I had never experienced. My bag was taken to my suite, and then we drove to the production office, where I was given five hundred dollars cash for pocket change!

Though I'd read the script, I didn't understand much of it, and the director and producer spent a lot of time coaching me. Storytelling was such a valued tradition and skill back home, and the narrative process involved in filmmaking appealed to me—it was something I wanted to master. I had searched for a way to tell my story. I'd felt that no one who wasn't a Lost Boy could possibly understand me. Yet I wanted so badly to be understood.

I put my heart and soul into the part. It wasn't a big role, but it meant the world, because I was able to let a bit of me out onscreen. And because some kids out there who looked like me might see me—find me—and hope for more for themselves.

THE MODEL LIFE

THE UNIVERSITY OF BRIDGEPORT HAD granted me a leave of absence to complete *I Heart Huckabees*. When it was released in 2004, entertainment professionals showed intense interest in me, so while finishing my bachelor's degree, I dedicated a chunk of my time to pursuing acting opportunities in New York, sensing a bigger, better role could be in the offing.

One morning, coming from an audition for a role in the movie *Inside Man,* my friend Randy from Brooklyn and I were walking around the Wall Street area when a stranger approached us from behind and started calling out.

STRANGER: Stop! Hey, stop, you two!

ME: I'm not from New York, so I can't help you with directions.

He was unrelenting and ran up to us.

STRANGER: Hey! Excuse me. May I please speak to you for a moment?

Randy and I stopped and turned around.

STRANGER: Hey! Sorry to disturb you. My name is Norman Watson. I'm a photographer.

RANDY: Well, Mr. Watson. How can we help you?

NORMAN: I wanted to speak to your friend here. I think he has a look I can use in an upcoming shoot.

I didn't understand what the man was going on about, but all of a sudden my friend seemed really interested. I still hadn't registered where this could lead, but Randy, acting like a hungry talent manager, took the man's business card and promised to be in touch in the next few days. As we walked on, Randy couldn't contain himself.

RANDY: This could be a huge opportunity. We need to follow it through and see where it leads!

Randy called me a few days later.

RANDY: Ger, I spoke to the guy we met on Wall Street. He's set up a shoot for you.

ME: What? He's setting up a shoot already?

RANDY: Yes. And you won't believe who he's doing the shoot for.

ME: Blow my mind, bro!

RANDY: The *Fader,* bro! Believe it or not.

ME: Get out of here!

RANDY: I kid you not.

I couldn't believe my luck. I knew of the *Fader,* a magazine that was the voice of young musicians, highlighting their lifestyles and world. I didn't imagine I could get a spread in it, just like that.

The day of the shoot, Randy and I went to the set. Norman told me he wanted the look and theme to be avant-garde, with an experimental, artistic side to it.

NORMAN: Bring as much of your personality out as possible.

That was his only instruction. He then started streaming some Caribbean music in the background.

NORMAN: Move along to it.

First, I went through the clothes on the rack and selected various outfits. Besides the Armanis and Cassinis, I wore retro zebra-print pants, a classic polo by Penguin, a Paul Smith hat, some cool things from David Owens Vintage Clothing, a shirt from Dries Van Noten, and pieces by John Bartlett. I stepped in front of the camera, closed my eyes, turned into someone else, and got lost in the world, moving my limbs around as Norman's long-lensed camera clicked away. Not being me was exhilarating but also exhausting: standing for long periods and twisting my body into knots. It wasn't the same as racing up and down the court, but somehow it took just as much focus and effort.

I was tired and sweaty by the time we called it a wrap, hours later. Norman invited Randy and me to his studio and ordered beer and pizza, and we became fast friends. We spoke about the latest trends and what the word was in the fashion industry's grapevine.

NORMAN: Oh, after this *Fader* shoot, Ger? I think you'll be killing it.

RANDY: Please don't forget us little people.

We all laughed, but I knew these guys were selling me a dream!

It took almost six months for the pictures to come out in the *Fader*. When they did, in a photo essay titled "Wrong Man," there was a rumbling in the fashion industry. People started talking about this new male model with accentuated African features.

I was in the meatpacking district with my friend Sy,

who was a model for Boss Models, when David Bossman, a highly respected man in fashion, approached me to sign with his agency.

> **DAVID**: Ger, why don't you join our agency? I am planning to put together a package in Milano this June. I think you can book a lot of jobs. We'll be your mother agency here in New York.

> **ME**: I'll think about it, David.

> **DAVID**: Here's my card. Don't be a stranger.

> **ME**: I don't meet strangers, David.

I got signed by Boss Models, becoming a catwalk sensation for a time: the tall, dark Sudanese male model who stood out in shows. I would even see people pointing at me on the streets of New York, something that had never happened before. This newly acquired recognition gave me professional traction. Either I was cast as the lead model opening the show, or I would be saved for last, to close it.

I was flooded with requests for photo shoots, to a point where I had to get choosy. I hadn't imagined a day would come, when my distinctly Nuer features, widely shared by my childhood friends and relatives, would be a source of pride and bring me a measure of fame and fortune, as opposed to derision.

In order to remain visible and keep a high profile in the business, my booking agent always told me, I had to show my face everywhere and immerse myself in the lifestyle. Thus, I became a social butterfly, attending Fashion's Night Out and lavish events for leading industry players like Gucci and Marc Jacobs, after which I would join friends at after-parties, then move on to club-hopping with prominent New York nightlife promoters.

But I was having trouble fully accepting that this was the ultimate life I was going to lead, since it felt like one long stage production, where you had to stick to your role, never deviating from the script. And hobnobbing with the industry's who's who while also attending college wasn't easy. I felt mentally and emotionally drained. This was so far removed from who I was growing up, who I thought I'd become, what I thought was important in life. It was fun, but it was fleeting. For someone who had always sought purpose, this seemed like a distraction. Yet it was a welcome one, given what I'd been through, and I wasn't going to give it up that easily.

PROMOTION

AS *EXCITING* AS *MODELING* WAS, it was also all-consuming. To recenter myself, I took a brief break and moved to Nebraska, where I worked at a Tyson plant. It was there that I learned from my cousin Wunbil that my father had gotten into a disagreement with Nyantek, Wunbil's mother, and killed her. My mind was in chaos and my body was powerless to turn back the hands of time to save her—to save anyone. More discord, disruption, and devastation from my real life was seeping into this one, the idealized fantasy version. I couldn't reconcile the two. I couldn't keep them apart.

I returned to New York City after a year and moved into an apartment in Washington Heights with Kueth's younger sister, Nok, with whom I'd lived in Bloomington. Tall, slim, and confident, Nok was a big encouragement, always urging me to take my modeling career more seriously.

NOK: You have what it takes to get an even bigger break in fashion, Ger.

She had gotten interested in fashion and was laying the groundwork for her own modeling career. Along with Nok in the apartment was Chi Chi, her friend from Georgetown University and an athlete of great note, with whom I became close.

Our three-bedroom apartment turned into a sort of mini United Nations, where dozens of friends, mostly in the fashion industry, from many different countries, would come and hang out. Nok, Chi Chi, and I introduced our friends to each other, and the fact that we all had outgoing personalities made any visitor feel at home. The apartment's kitchen was always busy, cuisines from across the world getting whipped up in there: Jamaican (jerk chicken), Haitian (black rice), Nigerian (the rice dish *jollof*), Sudanese (okra and combo stew), and African American (soul food, barbecue, sweet cornbread, and desserts).

By this time, I was starting to sort of build my life from scratch again, doing catering, waiting tables, and being a personal trainer, trying to save as much money as possible. But Nok had other ideas.

NOK: Ger, guess what!

ME: What?

NOK: I talked to my mom and dad in Juba. They want us to come back to Sudan.

Uncle Wal and Aunt Julia had already relocated from America back to Sudan, and were now serving as senior officials in the new interim government.

ME: Really?!

NOK: Yeah, there's more opportunity there than here in New York.

ME: But our country just got out of war a year ago through the Comprehensive Peace Agreement. We might be united under the name of Dr. John Garang Mabior, but that doesn't mean we've got prospects yet. Where do you think the country's going to get money?

NOK: It's oil money, dude!

I was so taken by my new life that I myself couldn't quite imagine going back home. Life in the fast lane was beckoning once again.

In time, I stopped doing the catering and restaurant jobs to focus exclusively on modeling. My new roommate, JAn Christiansen, and I settled into a simple routine. We "worked" all night at clubs across New York, got home in the morning totally exhausted, slept the whole day, woke up in the evening, hit the gym hard, got back to the apartment, made our one solid meal for the day, and jumped back into the nightlife all over again. On some crazy nights, the party would turn into a party-after-the-party at someone's apartment early in the morning. These sometimes lasted the whole day, meaning neither JAn nor I would get a chance to go back to our apartment. We would leave the party in the evening, hit the gym without failure, get a quick change of clothes along the way, then promptly report to the nightclub scene and carry on partying. That's what qualified as work, and we were paid by the club supervisors just to be there.

In the alluring swirl of all this glitz and glamour of nights surrounded by some of the most beautiful people in New York, at some of the hottest nightlife destinations with the bass thumping and the champagne flowing, I almost managed to forget my past sorrows. I unwittingly put aside my professor uncle and aunt's intellectual aspirations for me. I allowed my concerns and curiosity about the fates of my family members back in Sudan to completely fade into the background. That's the power of life in the fast lane, bright lights and endless partying. It was fantasy, an escape. And I was running from my demons, fleeing my past as I'd had to do my whole life. But, eventually, reality always catches up to you.

Although this was my job—yes, partying was my work—I didn't feel peace or calm inside. It was as though the only way not to have to face myself in the mirror (ironic, given that the lifestyle is all about looks) was to keep going, to keep partying, to keep waking up at one more model's apartment, without ever taking a break. Because in the quiet is when the nightmares start to scream.

NEAR MISS

MY COUSINS NOK AND KUETH finally convinced me to visit Sudan with my father's eldest son, my half brother Ruot, who was also living in America.

> **KUETH**: We can find more cutting-edge facilities to train in, since they're starting from the ground up.

> **ME**: Last I was there, we all lived in the bush. You're trying to tell me it's gonna be more advanced there than it is here?

> **KUETH**: Let's find out!

One evening in January 2008, while watching TV at a coffee shop in Union Square, I saw images of burning buildings and barricaded roads on CNN. The reporter was giving a detailed account of the violence rocking Kenya following a disputed presidential election. Our trip back to

Sudan was supposed to take us through Kenya. We had already bought our tickets.

In the coming days, the State Department warned Americans against going to Kenya. Nok opted out of the trip because of the new developments. We supported her decision.

The rest of us decided to disregard the travel advisory and make the trip. We took a six-hour flight on American Airlines from JFK to Heathrow in London, where we hopped on our connecting flight to Jomo Kenyatta International Airport in Nairobi.

The flight to Kenya had barely twenty passengers aboard the massive plane. Everyone had an entire row of seats to themselves. When we landed, we went to a hotel at the edge of the city center. From my experience as a child of war, I could tell just by looking in people's eyes that something wasn't right. I woke up early the following morning, reminiscing about the time I flew from Nairobi to JFK through Frankfurt. I opened the curtain and saw long lines of people walking to work, possibly low-wage earners who couldn't afford to stay home even when the country was burning. The public parks below my window were full of military personnel and armored vehicles on standby, anticipating trouble.

We stayed in Nairobi for two more days before departing for Juba, southern Sudan's seat of power, which I had never been to before. Three years after the Comprehensive Peace Agreement was signed on January 9, 2005, ending the war between us southerners and the Arab-dominated government in Khartoum and establishing a democratic governance so that southern and northern Sudan could share oil revenue, there was now talk all across southern Sudan of separation and the formation of a new republic. The agreement had allowed for a six-year grace period, after which a referendum would be held to decide whether the south wanted to remain part of Sudan or become a new nation, South Sudan. Juba would be its capital.

When we landed in Juba, I saw that my people now had an actual functioning airport, which they serviced themselves. It was nothing like Jomo Kenyatta or Heathrow, but I was amazed to see so many different airlines coming in and out. I never thought I would see an end to the Sudanese civil wars, let alone development and modernization take their place. My uncle Wal and aunt Julia were waiting for us at the airport, surrounded by lots of people, some who spoke to me in Nuer like we'd met before. I let the feeling rising inside me wash over me: I was home.

On our ride in a four-wheel-drive Land Cruiser, I saw as much construction as I did abandoned military tanks. We approached my uncle's gated compound, where plastic chairs had already been set up, and where he had to introduce me, his son Kueth, and my elder (half) brother Ruot to Duany, whom I hadn't seen in over a decade and a half.

ME: Hey, Duany!

I shouted to him before I even got out of the vehicle.

DUANY: Ger!

The moment the vehicle stopped, I jumped out and hugged him. We had each grown taller, but nothing else about our physical appearances seemed to have changed in the decade and a half since I'd seen him. I wanted to ask Duany one question. So after Kueth, Ruot, and I had been welcomed into the house and prayed for, and after my uncle had proudly introduced us as his children who had just arrived from America, I pulled Duany aside.

ME: How is Mum, Duany?

I spoke to him in Nuer. And, man, did that feel good.

ME: How can I get to see her?

DUANY: Ger, Mum is in Akobo. But don't think things here are calm. I don't think you can go to see her. There's a lot of sectarian killing going on.

It was unimaginable for me to come to Sudan and not see my mother. But the situation on the ground, with the warring communities, made the trip to the village untenable. In under a week, word that I was in Juba got to my mother in Akobo, and she dispatched my little brother Both to come see me. He was now twenty-one, with my brother Duany's facial features, but shorter. Both took a few days on the road, eventually showing up at my uncle's house in Juba.

BOTH: Ger, Mum heard that you are in Sudan. She sent me to confirm it was true.

ME: Yes, as you see, I'm here. I'll give you some things to take to her.

I wanted to send my mother some proof of life, and so I did some shopping, packed some photos of me in America together with some money, and gave them to Both to take to her.

ME: Tell Mum I won't go back to America before I see her.

A few days later, Uncle Wal and some government officials were going on a trip to a place near the Akobo region. I insisted on accompanying him, against his wishes.

UNCLE WAL: Ger, this place has changed. It's no longer how it was when you left. I am not even sure you can drink the water or eat the food and not have your stomach get upset.

In my head, I thought my uncle was kidding, because this was where I had come from.

ME: I will be fine, Uncle. I assure you nothing will happen to me.

In the end, my uncle gave in, letting me accompany him and his government colleagues on the journey on a shuttle flight. I was seated next to soldiers my age, some who had never flown before. They panicked every time the ride got bumpy, and I had to hold some of their guns. I sat there thinking this could have been me had things taken even the slightest turn in my life. I felt lucky. My intention was to get as close as possible to Akobo, then sneak away and visit my mother. But when we got to the villages my uncle was visiting, we were informed of intense communal fighting in the surrounding villages, making it impossible for me to venture farther. It would be a two-day walk to Akobo. I couldn't believe I was going back to New York without seeing Mum. War was ripping us apart again. I couldn't escape it here, there, anywhere. And it was tearing me up inside.

A MEANINGFUL LIFE

THE MOMENT I GOT BACK to New York in May, I realized something had fundamentally changed inside me. I went back to my apartment and my roommate, JAn, then tried hitting the nightclub scene with a bevy of beautiful models in tow, but none of it was exciting anymore. I would catch myself sitting alone, quiet, deep in thought. Sudan, my mother, and my family took up more room inside my mind, and JAn couldn't figure out who I had become either.

JAN: What is going on with you, Ger? You're not yourself.

ME: I think the opposite is true. I wasn't myself before. No one who does what we do is.

I started focusing more on fitness and got a job as a personal trainer at New York Sports Clubs. I reported for work at four a.m. every day and left for home at five p.m., and in the evenings, I went to acting and modeling castings. This strict routine became my new life.

I started saving the money I earned, hoping to fund a documentary about my life in Sudan and America. I soon shared the idea with a number of my Hollywood contacts. Meanwhile, I revisited my earlier plan of going to Milan, Italy, and staying for a few months to model.

Arrangements were made with an agency in Milan to act as my local host there. No sooner had I put foot to pavement that June than I was surrounded by hundreds of models, makeup artists, and other human cogs in the fashion industry, all chasing designers, casting directors, and agency representatives, hunting for gigs.

Each evening in Milan, we gathered to drink cheap wine, talk, and dance. I became friends with an African American model named Ibrahim Baaith, who had a Black Panthers background and always got deep, trying to focus the conversation on the need for more consciousness in the world: mainly about slavery, the ills of capitalism, and the oppression of black people across the world.

Ibrahim liked asking me about Africa and Sudan, wanting me to take more of an interest in what was happening there. We were usually the only blacks present at these nightly outings, and Ibrahim always focused his attention on my journey from Africa, emphasizing how far I had traveled as a refugee to be part of the fashion industry. Our conversations lit a spark inside me and gave me a sense of direction in my search for a meaningful life.

Ibrahim returned to New York about a week later, and in his absence, I cut down on the late-night, cheap-wine-drinking routine and spent more time working out in public parks, where I would see black people, mostly immigrants, with nowhere to stay. Sometimes during my public workouts, small crowds would gather around to watch me. That's how I started speaking and opening up to the black people.

I saw firsthand the hard lives lived by these African refugees in Italy, many of whom were homeless and shared stories of how they endured terrible racism on the Italian streets. Here, it was out in the open and on the surface, whereas in America, the racism is baked into the earth, woven into its fabric to the point where you can overlook it if you don't know how to spot the threads. These people, who looked so similar to me, squatted in the streets, sleeping on cardboard. While my fellow models whisked past such scenes, minding their business on the way to the next party or runway show, I couldn't help but think about my late brother Chuol, who'd possibly suffered the same fate in Addis Ababa before dying a miserable, lonely death. There was a thin line separating me from these less fortunate refugees, a fact that made me detest the self-centered life I had thrived in for most of my twenties. It had to come to an end. I also felt a burning desire to lift up other refugees, the way my aunt and uncle had done for me.

The combination of the suffering I saw in Milan and my cousin Nok constantly mentioning our homeland inspired me to want to turn my life's focus toward activism, for the benefit of those who had traveled journeys like mine but maybe gone off the rails. At that point—at an incredible career high—I realized how lucky I had been. I understood on a deep level that even as the refugee resettlement program had saved the lives of innumerable people like myself, we still suffered crippling emotional damage as a result of being cut off from our pasts and cultures. I had always felt an incredible sense of kinship whenever I spent time with other refugees—a feeling of affiliation—and I wanted to preserve and share that with the entire African diaspora, emotionally removed from its roots.

I reached out to my southern Sudanese friend Ajou Deng, from our Lost Boys team in Connecticut, who now lived in London, and asked him whether I could stop over on my way to New York. I bought a one-way ticket to London.

I landed at Gatwick Airport and received the shock of my life. Immigration officials pulled me aside, as if I were a criminal, and started interrogating me and checking my luggage.

IMMIGRATION OFFICIAL: What's your name?

ME: Ger Duany.

IMMIGRATION OFFICIAL: Where are you from?

ME: I'm originally from Sudan.

IMMIGRATION OFFICIAL: Why are you traveling around Europe . . . and carrying an American passport?

ME: I am an American citizen of Sudanese origin. I am a model. I'm coming from doing modeling gigs in Milan.

IMMIGRATION OFFICIAL: Why are you in London?

ME: I'm here to visit my friend Ajou.

IMMIGRATION OFFICIAL: We don't believe anything you say. You must return to Milan on the next flight out of London.

I couldn't believe it.

Back in Milan, airport authorities picked me off the plane as if I were some high-profile international criminal. I explained to them what I had been doing in Milan before flying out to London, and gave them the address of where I had been staying. They let me go. I went back to the apartment the agency had rented for me, but it was already late at night. The landlord couldn't hear me knock. That night I slept outside on the streets, at a bus stop.

The following morning, I returned to the apartment.

LANDLORD: Ger, I thought you had left for London?

I spared him the details of my trip.

I flew back to New York at the end of July. I became a complete recluse, more than I already had been. I pulled away from fashion and modeling for a bit and focused on what was happening back in Sudan. I started using any platform to write and share my thoughts, and people who knew me began to notice my transformation—and to pay attention.

JAn remarked on the intensity of my conversations and how my outlook had completely changed. I used to clown around a lot—a social butterfly—but now, he and others said, I moved with a purpose. I have no idea how they picked up on so much just through my body language. People who weren't familiar with me or my work also started getting drawn to the things I was talking about and working on. I realized there was traction and interest in what I was doing.

For the next two years, I worked as a high-end personal trainer in New York while living in an apartment my cousin Kueth had left me in Harlem. I continued to turn down modeling jobs and plugged myself into the network of Sudanese activists across the world. I was becoming someone else in the eyes of those who knew me, and there was no turning back.

Over the previous ten years, Paul and my aunt and uncle had been back to Sudan several times. Each time any of them made the trip, it felt to me like they were going all the way to the moon. After my disastrous flight to London, and with the difficulty I had experienced just making ends meet, the thought of flying to Sudan again filled me with a lot of fear. But now it dawned on me that as an American citizen, I had the right to come and go from America as I pleased. I could return to Sudan without risking being caught up in the dead end of war and starvation. I had citizenship, which I'd taken my time applying for—I waited almost a decade—because although I had one foot in the United States, the other was still firmly rooted in Sudan. I also now had money, which allowed me to do something as simple as visit my father. I resolved to do just that as soon as I could.

My trip to Milan had given me a different perspective. My new brother, Ibrahim, who told me I had opened his eyes to Africa, had awakened something new, something important inside me. I wanted to create a life with meaning.

PICTURE-IMPERFECT

I BUMPED INTO A FRIEND, the southern Sudanese rapper and activist Emmanuel Jal, during an event in New York City sometime around the summer of 2010.

We met up for a quick drink at sunset on the rooftop of a boutique hotel on the East Side, where we had a long conversation about what we could do about the situation back home. The fighting between Sudan's north and south had finally ceased, and by this time the two warring parties were heading toward the referendum required by the terms of the Comprehensive Peace Agreement. The vote was to allow citizens of the south of Sudan to make a choice between keeping Sudan united and splitting from the north to form an independent state, South Sudan.

ME: Can you believe South Sudan may be the world's newest nation this year?

EMMANUEL: Yeah, bro, we'll make sure we raise the flag, because the distance between the north and south will be vast, like between the earth and the piercing sky.

ME: I am so high in spirit. I want us to mobilize the lost boys and girls worldwide to participate in a summit in East Africa. I want to prove we are not lost, we are finding our way back to our home and are united as one people.

EMMANUEL: Yes, this is big, bruh. I'll talk to David Nyuol in Australia. He's a community organizer. You reach out to Valentino Achak Deng in Kenya.

Emmanuel and I settled on holding a fundraiser and a few other events that would bring together the lost boys and girls of Sudan, culminating in a summit in Nairobi. The goal was to capture the attention of Sudanese government officials and make them interact with the younger exiled population. We managed to raise over thirty thousand pounds and finally had a unified, audible voice.

After the summit, I decided that the best thing for me to do was to return to Sudan to make my documentary film about my experiences, complicated and improbable as they were. Coming from where I came from, having done the things I ended up doing, I knew my life story read like fiction, yet I was of the view that, given a chance, a lot more Sudanese youth could soar even higher than I had.

There was no telling whether I would be able to find my mother and father, not to mention my stepmothers and surviving siblings: my elder brother Duany, my younger sister Nyakuar, and my younger brothers Both and Gok. And if I did find them, would Nyakuar and Both still recognize me after spending so many years apart? Would they know my face, and would they know what was underneath that face, and within my heart?

I thought of my childhood friends too, whom I hadn't heard from or about in so many years—Gol Tut Khor, who had been so tiny and defenseless. Or Jangjuol, whose sunken face the day Paul sent him back to Akobo I had never forgotten. Or Garang Barjok, with whom I took karate lessons and play-fought in Itang.

The SPLA provided my group a charter flight from Nairobi's Wilson Airport to Juba, their main condition being that we register to vote in the upcoming referendum, as well as ask more of our fellow lost boys and girls to do the same from wherever they were across the world. My Kenyan filmmaker friend, Wanuri Kahiu, carried a tiny hidden camera, recording every bit of my trip as we went along. Trying to look formal and present a serious face, we wore suits, only to land in Juba and come face to face with the blistering sun. The SPLA had heavily mobilized its supporters to receive us and had a huge reception party, complete with traditional dancers led by a spear-wielding warrior, in the airport's VIP section. We were then taken to the mausoleum of Dr. John Garang (who had died in a helicopter crash in 2005), which had become a huge symbol of my people's struggle for liberation.

• • •

After our meeting with the SPLA representatives, Emmanuel Jal, Valentino Achak Deng, and David Nyuol opted to stay on in Juba with my filmmaking friends to visit my uncle Wal and aunt Julia, who, as senior government officials, were readying the south for what was clearly imminent independence.

At their compound, I met my little brother Gok and cousin Nok. Seeing eighteen-year-old Gok—just an infant when I had left Sudan—was a revelation. To him, I had never been anything but a mythical figure: brother Ger, who killed an antelope at age six, who fought off cattle rustlers with an AK-47, who supported Mum whenever Dad left her in anger or in war, who flew to America and graduated from high school. I was a legend, larger than life. Someone he'd only heard of in stories. His Oder.

GOK: I saw the two hundred dollars that you sent. I'd never seen American money before. Mum kept the money for over a year. Every now and then, she pulled the money out of the box and we'd look at it, but we didn't have any use for it in Akobo.

ME: I should have thought of that.

GOK: But the year we walked to the Gambella region, we were rich all of a sudden. We couldn't believe the exchange rate. We helped everyone in the neighborhood with it.

ME: With two hundred dollars? The whole neighborhood?

I had forgotten how rich America was compared to so many other countries. That pocket change from a movie shoot could feed and clothe a village.

I enjoyed listening to my brother and was fascinated by his mature approach to life. For the most part, I kept silent during our conversation. Deep down in my heart, I knew time had slipped away from us.

MY OWN MAN

WE LANDED IN MALAKAL, OUR first stopover on our trip to Akobo. Wanuri and our director of photography, Marius van Graan, had both fallen sick with stomach issues, but we pressed on. My goal was to get to see my father this trip and I would not let anything stop me.

Trucks were parked all over the place, thousands of southerners moving back from the north, carrying all their belongings. Everyone now anticipated the separation of Sudan into two independent countries. People were sitting in groups, talking about what to expect once the south gained its independence from the north. We moved around and spoke to a number of them, drinking tea in open-air spots along the road, about what this moment and movement meant for them and their families.

Wanuri, who was light-skinned and had covered herself up like a Muslim, easily passed for a northerner. Marius, who was a white South African, made us appear like a group of foreign agents on a mission. I therefore had to intervene, explaining to my southern countrymen who we were and what we were up to, whenever we encountered some resistance.

We stayed in Malakal for close to a week, the main reason being the delay in getting clearance to visit my father. He was the equivalent of a prisoner on death row in America. When I finally made headway with the prison authorities, I went in with Wanuri, who was to record our first interaction. We were received by an overenthusiastic guard, who looked at me expectantly, as if we were supposed to know each other from somewhere. But I couldn't figure out where.

GUARD: Ger, you don't recognize me? It's Gol!

ME: Oh my God! Gol, look at you!

I couldn't believe this was the tiny and defenseless friend with whom I'd played out on the fields of the Itang refugee camp in Ethiopia in the late 1980s. He had since become a muscled powerhouse of a man, risen to the rank of major in the Sudan police force, and married four wives. Despite the devastating reason why I was visiting the prison, we both rejoiced at our reunion. How far apart fate had taken us children of Sudan! Yet we were still able to reconnect, albeit under excruciating circumstances, and share a moment of joy.

Gol took me to meet his boss, the prison superintendent,

who was to give final authorization for me to see my father. He did so and, after some negotiation, also agreed to let us use a camera.

The moment my father was brought in, the entire room went dead silent. He wore a formerly white but now dingy shirt, brown khaki pants, and plain flip-flops. He was chained at both the wrists and ankles, causing the stout old man to drag himself slowly across the room, a thoroughly humiliating exercise for him and a devastating spectacle for me. It was the first time I had ever seen my proud warrior father subdued, powerless. I felt the humiliation he had brought upon himself fill the room.

DAD: *HELLO, ALL!*

My father greeted everyone in his familiar, roaring voice. He then sat down slowly before lifting his head and looking around to see if he could recognize anyone. I waited to see if he'd remember me, but he didn't. As always, never one to cede ground, especially when he felt he had a chance to assert himself, my father took charge of the gathering.

DAD: They say I am here to meet someone who has come to visit me all the way from America. But I only have two people in America. Two of my sons. My eldest son, Ruot, and my younger son Ger.

Not wanting to prolong the awkwardness in the room, I took this as my cue to step forward.

ME: Dad, this is your son Ger.

I spoke to him in Nuer, standing up to embrace him, getting all teary.

But before I could even get to my father, the prison superintendent interrupted, realizing by this time that Wanuri was capturing this special moment. The superintendent seemed to imagine my friends were a television crew and now wanted to address them and become the center of attention.

SUPERINTENDENT: This man here is my brother-in-law.

He pointed at my father. Then he pointed at me.

SUPERINTENDENT: This one here is my nephew. Let me now tell you about the problems of Sudan.

He was changing his tune, acting as though he were fond of my father and me. But before he could go any further, Wanuri, who had some guts, interrupted him.

WANURI: I'm sorry. We're not here to listen to you, but rather to capture the special moment when this father and son reunite.

The superintendent backed off, embarrassed.

There was no privacy for us to have a real father-and-son conversation, and so we quickly exchanged pleasantries and made do with the few minutes we had, touching base in the most superficial way after having been apart for nearly two decades.

DAD: I am proud of you and what you have made of yourself despite being out there alone. I feel like I owe you and your brothers, sisters, and mothers so much that I don't know if I will ever be able to make it up to all of you. But here I am now. There's little I can do. But I am proud of you, Ger. Always remember that. You have done well for yourself.

This was a profoundly emotional moment for me, listening to my father, with whom I'd last interacted as we sought to avenge my sister Nyandit's death. I had become my own man, and now my father seemed to be looking up to me, after all my life everyone had looked up to him.

ME: I hear you, Dad. You know we still need you despite everything that's happened. We are still your children and your family.

DAD: Go and tell Wunbil and his sisters that bitterness will not resolve anything. I know I killed their mother, but my death from hanging and the hatred the family might feel for me will not solve anything. Tell them I am here carrying my cross, and this should settle the matter. I will carry my own cross. Don't let my actions in rage break the family apart.

It was hard to gauge whether my father was being remorseful or defiant, since he had always been a hard man to read, never expressive. Nothing had changed. It was as if he still wanted to be in charge, yet was also relinquishing control. Short, with a bushy beard and balding head, he looked like a blood brother to Dr. John Garang. I had now grown much taller than he, but his voice still had an authority about it, a power over me, taking me back to the days of my childhood in Akobo, when I would ask to clean his gun for him as an act of loyalty and responsibility, committing to his way of life as a young boy.

I then asked my father to speak directly to the camera and say something about his life or whatever he felt was important. In that moment, I saw my father become the man I had always known him to be: poised and authoritative, roaring in self-belief. Everyone in the room kept quiet, waiting to hear what the once indomitable Thabach Duany, now a chained-up guest of the state, had to say.

DAD: This land where you see me now imprisoned is a land that I fought for from the time I was nineteen years old. John Garang and I fought the Arabs using bare rocks. That is how long I've been fighting for this land with my two bare hands.

We were mesmerized by what he was saying.

DAD: Ger, I want you to listen to me. Go and tell all your mothers—my wives—and all your brothers and sisters that they must go and vote. Tell them to vote for separation. You must all vote for separation so that our people and our land can be free, once and for all.

That moment, now quiet and attentive, felt like my father was speaking to all of southern Sudan, oscillating between the personal and the not personal, using our family as a metaphor for Sudan. My father, in a low-pitched voice, continued:

DAD: I know your heart is heavy and you have carried a lot of burdens for a lot of people for many years. I heard you came in 2008 but couldn't see us. But now you're back. All these things you see me going through now, this imprisonment, don't matter to me. Do you know how few people from my generation are still alive? I am lucky to still be here.

My father was passing the baton to me. He spent a lot of time talking about the future, telling me that whatever he and his generation had faced was nothing, asking that I and my brothers and sisters get ready for an even tougher time ahead.

DAD: We are just turning over a new leaf, which doesn't come with any guarantees.

My dad's need for unity within the family seemed to be as important to him as the future of Sudan. To him, unity between Wunbil, myself, and my siblings was non-negotiable.

DAD: What you and Wunbil and everyone else must be thinking about is the future. The kind of price your generation is going to pay may be higher than what my generation had to pay. I know Wunbil is angry at me because I shot his mother. But do you know how many people we have all killed from the time we started fighting for freedom until now? We have even killed each other as we fought the north. But the time has come to start afresh. Tell that to your brother Wunbil when you go back to America. And remember to vote for separation, son.

I felt a mixture of emotions as our time to leave came. On the one hand, I was angry that my father had brought all this upon himself, and that now the family had to deal with the aftereffects of his rage. But on the other hand, I was just a son looking at his father, meeting him for the first time in ages. Had I stayed on a soldier's path, this could have been me. I could have taken who knows how many lives of my "enemies" or even my family and friends. Or they might have taken mine in such a chaotic society.

ME: I have heard you, Dad. But I want you to know that no one can put things back together but you. Three years ago, I came here but couldn't make it home to Akobo. I returned to America and now I'm back. I will go to Akobo and deliver your message. I am happy that I have seen you this time. I know you are a strong man.

That visit would remain an indelible memory, as if I had left a part of me at the prison in Malakal and taken a part of my father out with me.

SEPARATION

AT THE TIME, THE ONLY way to Akobo from Malakal was by speedboat down the Nile. I was cautioned that this meant passing through volatile territory, where there was fighting. The fact that Wanuri and Marius were visibly foreign meant that we would become automatic targets for attack and extortion.

I called my mother from Malakal, where I was sitting on the bank of the Nile. I told her I had come as far as Malakal, but getting back to Akobo was proving difficult.

MUM: My son, if this is really your voice that I am hearing, then that's enough for me. Don't make the mistake of coming through the Nile. You will be risking the lives of the people you are with. I have heard your voice. That is enough for me for now.

Our only option was to head back to Juba and wait for the plane that flew once a week from there through Bor to the greater Akobo area. We paid for a ride on a humanitarian helicopter from Malakal to Juba, where we stayed in a little makeshift hotel, tents erected next to the Nile. Two days later, we took the thirty-minute flight to Bor before proceeding to Akobo. Throughout the trip, all that was on my mind was my mother, how she was doing, and how she might look after nearly two decades apart.

By the time we arrived, the landing strip was filled with people waiting to see the long-gone Ger. There was jubilation, and the area's government representative sent an armed guard to keep watch over my friends and me for as long as we stayed in Akobo. As I traveled through the countryside—where every tree, hut, and field of grass seemed hauntingly familiar—I saw deep creases of long-held rage on the faces of my countrymen and women. Generations of war had changed our culture forever, but not, I hoped, beyond repair. Despite all the suffering, there was optimism that a new nation would rise from the chaos and bloodshed.

After much wandering across the world, searching, I'd finally gotten back to Akobo. It didn't look so different. I couldn't exactly recall the direction of my home, but the people who had received me at the landing strip were already leading the way.

It was a homecoming like I'd never imagined. We arrived at a homestead, which brought back a torrent of memories, and that was when I knew I was home. Women and children were all over us, and I couldn't tell who was who.

ME: Where's my mother. Does anyone know?

I sat under a familiar tree in front of my mother's grass-thatched hut, not believing I had finally set foot in Akobo after so many years. A gentle breeze swept through the dusty town, and suddenly there she was—my tall, proud mother. To my delight, when she saw me, her face held nothing but joy. She was slender in body, but her alignment was not the same. It had been about eighteen years since we'd last seen each other.

MUM: Are you really Ger, who came out of my womb? Should I scream? Should I sing? Tell me what to do!

At first, my mother wouldn't even touch me. She walked around the compound as though she were possessed by some invisible powers, chanting something inaudible, sneaking glances at me, and wondering aloud whether it was really me. In the end, she went into her hut and brought out a gourd of water, which she sprinkled all around me, and on my head, as she chanted a traditional prayer.

MUM: In God's name, blessings to you all. Blessings to my son and his guests.

She then washed my hands. It was only after performing these rituals that she finally touched me, her hands trembling, tears dancing in her eyes, her face creased with a mixture of joy and sadness. I remained still and surrendered myself to my mother, who studied the physical presence of a son she'd spent countless sleepless nights worrying about, a son who had gone into the unknown and emerged as though back from the dead, safe and sound.

I kept smiling, though I was overcome by sadness at having been away from my mother and my siblings for too many years. I felt deep down that maybe I could have been protecting them, fending for them. Yet, at the same time, I felt a sense of relief, as if this was exactly how everything was supposed to have turned out. More importantly, my dominant emotion was gratitude, for everything. I had come from this village, this homestead, I had traveled the world, and I was lucky enough to have found my way back home, right into my mother's arms, even as she had grown frail. I felt whole, joyful, and safe again.

I watched my mother the entire time before I moved my hands and touched her back, standing up to embrace her. I had not felt her warmth in nearly twenty years, and this was easily the most emotional moment of my adult life. I was weak but strong, certain but confused, and I knew I wanted to be nowhere else but right there in her arms, as though I were once again a little boy needing her guidance and protection.

Once the initial excitement subsided, my mother started in with the questions.

MUM: Where have you been and what have you been up to all these years you've been away?

I proudly told her all about my life—being a refugee, moving to America, going to school, modeling—and everything I had accomplished. She didn't understand the notion of getting paid to wear clothes, but all that mattered to her was that she was looking at her grown-up son.

My mother then walked me to her hut. I had once sent her two photos of me in America, and there they were, in her simple mud hut, proudly displayed, eaten slightly with age. She took them down, saying all she recognized from them was my teeth and eyes, that my body had changed.

MUM: I used to tell people that I really don't know if this is my son. And maybe he had become a runaway renegade like his long-lost uncle Machiel Duany.

We burst out laughing.

Two bulls were slaughtered that day, one from my father's side of the family, and another from my mother's side, in line with tradition. My uncle Reat was almost assuming the role of my father now, seeing that there was no other male figure in the home to take care of the traditional rites of welcoming me.

I then brought up the story of my father.

ME: How do you all think he is doing? Or his other wives and their children?

That's when my mother's smile faded, her face turning sad. Not knowing that I had already seen him, Mum spoke up.

MUM: If you want to see your father, you have to put in a request at the prison in Malakal, where he is being held.

ME: I've actually been there to see him.

Seeing my mother's sadness brought a surge of anger in me, and my heart broke once again, thinking of Mama Nyantek's death. Here I was, witnessing the consequences of his actions, a torn and haunted family that had a heavy, dark cloud hanging over it.

Seated there with the family, I decided to relay my father's message to them. I had recorded his words using my cell phone, and after telling my mothers and siblings that he wanted them to vote for separation, I asked them to sit still before I played my father's prison speech.

When I turned on the recording, the whole room erupted into wild cheers of surprise, few able to believe they were once again hearing my father speak right in front of them. In that moment of chaos, my mother took away the phone, running into an inner room with my second auntie Nyagieng so they could have a moment with their husband. It was a hilarious sight.

MUM: Is Thabach really speaking?

NYAGIENG: Yes, that's really his voice!

As my mothers took their turns listening to the recording in private, those left behind in the room with me were awestruck, with all conversation dominated by Nuer exclamations. I now understood how much clout my father still had in the family.

Once my mothers brought back the phone, I was asked to replay my father's voice again, with everyone present forming a tight circle around me. I took the opportunity to be my father's emissary once again, relaying his thoughts to the family. This time around, anyone who attempted to interrupt the listening party was asked to keep quiet. When it concluded, it was back to exclamations. Some were shouting, some sat still, while my mothers gave me a longing look, as if they wanted me to play the recording once more. I told everyone I would preserve the recording, and that they could listen to it for as long as I was around. My father's message seemed to have hit home.

My mother had given my filmmaker friends a warm welcome, ensuring that her son's guests had the best that Akobo had to offer, treating them like they were her own children. An unfamiliar young child ran into the hut and into my mum's embrace, renewing her joy. All these kids, my mother explained, were my sister Nyakuar's! She was in a distant village, where she was staying with her inherited husband. Her first husband had been killed during the war, and for the time being, Mum was taking care of her seven children. I was amazed to think that my little sister, who had escorted me on my last journey out of Akobo, was now a mother, and such a fertile one at that. My mother told me my little brother Both was now an SPLA soldier, and even though the cease-fire with Khartoum was holding, he was on standby, just in case. I never got to see him or Nyakuar on that visit, but Mum encouraged me to go to Juba, where my only remaining older brother, Duany, was in the hospital, dying of pneumonia. I knew I would be back in Juba in under a week and would at least have a moment to check on him and see if there was anything I could do to save him.

Three days later, on January 9, 2011, I took all my surviving mothers and siblings to cast their vote in Akobo, a final gesture to honor my father's legacy. We felt like one large family once again, walking together, me holding my mother's hand.

My mother had never voted before, and she stared at her ballot for a long time—not because she didn't know what to do, but because the weight of being able to vote and have a say in her future had finally landed on her. As she dropped her ballot in the box, I could swear she stood a little taller, her hands got a little stronger. Something had lifted and changed her. Pride? Hope? Power? I think so. Like she was the mother of a new nation.

I spent an extra day with my mother in Akobo, just thankful to be able to be in her presence. We reminisced about the long treks we made during my childhood, and my mother couldn't express how grateful she was that I had managed to survive all those years and make something of myself. She was the one person who could give me the strength to carry on for the next phase of my life. The moments we shared before I left Akobo, eating the food she prepared and talking late into the night, would sustain me. And coming back home had changed me once again: something inside me had settled or lit up, as though I had just remembered how to be alive, and how to live life.

I had arrived in Juba on the last day of voting, and was the last person to vote (my voting station was next to Dr. Garang's mausoleum). I was there to witness the historic occasion and celebrate alongside my countrymen. Finally, out of the years of war and suffering for my people had arisen a new republic. But as my father had warned me when I visited him in prison, the price my generation would have to pay might be higher than that paid by his. South Sudan became an independent nation on July 9, 2011. And judging by what would unfold in South Sudan not even half a decade after independence, it seems my father's words were prophetic.

But this was a moment of victory. Seeing that my presence had brought everyone together, and that the palpable, genuine camaraderie among all my father's wives was spilling over to us, the siblings, gave me hope for the future. I knew that I had a role to play not only in bringing my family together (after some internal talks, my family resolved the murder case against my father and he was released in 2012—he currently lives in Akobo and is still deeply invested in the civil war there), but in midwifing peaceful coexistence among my countrymen, wherever I was.

I still don't have answers about why some of my family, my friends, or my countrymen survived while others didn't. I certainly cannot say why I ended up leading this life when so many others just as deserving (maybe more), just as smart (maybe more), just as brave (maybe more), just as determined (maybe more) had theirs extinguished in a hail of bullets or by indifferent destitution. All I can offer is that I could not allow my childhood traumas to defeat me in adulthood. And that I permitted myself to accept my past, after at first fleeing from it, and to build upon it, after at first denying it. It freed me from demons, both real and imagined, that can be found in any country, rich or poor. It has allowed me to be a source of inspiration and strength for others and given my life purpose and my suffering meaning. I look toward the future with happiness, hope, and excitement, because having climbed my way out of and faced all that is my past, I know I can face and surmount any obstacle life tosses me.

EPILOGUE

EPILOGUE

IN JUBA, I'D VISITED MY elder brother in the hospital and learned he could be cured were he in a more advanced institution like the one in Nairobi. I flew him there, where he received lifesaving treatment. I felt incredibly grateful that the weird worlds of fashion, acting, and clubbing had afforded me the means to do so. It was one of my first acts of putting my money where my mouth was. I'd gotten a taste of it and now I wanted to do more.

The fashion industry was instrumental in helping me raise an additional twenty-nine thousand dollars through Kickstarter right off the bat. CNN's *Inside Africa* program did a feature on me, which compelled even more South Sudanese nationals to pay attention to whatever I was involved in, most notably my initiatives toward peace in Sudan. And I continued to raise money for my documentary.

Back in New York, out of the blue, I bumped into Brownica, a friend and fellow South Sudanese model living and working in the city. She had recommended me for an acting gig in an upcoming movie. I got home to find the script for *The Good Lie* already there and my girlfriend in the middle of reading it.

From the very first page, I felt that this was something I wanted to be part of. It had a kind of emotional and psychological pull on my entire being. The script spoke to me, from the storyline to the sentiment, and the characters came to me naturally. The entire movie was playing out right before my eyes, as if I had been involved in its conception. It was while reading the script that I remembered a conversation I'd had ten years ago with Bobby Newmyer, a producer of *Training Day*, about doing this exact kind of movie. Unfortunately, Bobby had passed away before we could act on it.

I started walking around the apartment, moving from one room to the other, as though possessed by some spirit. I went into the bathroom, locked myself up, looked in the mirror, and, deep in thought, faced my reflection. I then walked out and stood in the middle of the lounge area, seeing and feeling myself acting out a scene, revisiting a familiar moment of a life I'd once lived. If anyone had been watching me at that moment, they would probably have thought I'd completely lost my mind.

The script had triggered something in both my mind and my body, and I knew no other way of dealing with it. Luckily, I was now alone in the apartment, as my girlfriend had left to run errands, so I had the freedom to act crazy. The moment I came back to my senses, I opened my computer and saw a new email alert. Mindy Marin, the movie's casting director, had written to me, introducing herself and telling me they had been looking for actors and, having received numerous recommendations on my behalf, were interested in speaking to me.

We talked on the phone, and she mentioned that the film starred Reese Witherspoon. I did not know who that was, which seemed to excite Mindy even more! I quickly auditioned for the three roles for Sudanese men, and my audition tapes were sent to Philippe Falardeau, the movie's director.

After a couple of days of anxious waiting, I received an email asking me to contact Philippe immediately. I took a break at my job at an Equinox gym and made a Skype call. Philippe and I instantly hit it off, the way Mindy and I had.

He told me that in 1994, while I left Akobo on my journey for America, he was getting caught in the crossfire between the two SPLA rival camps in Torit and Nasir while on a visit.

I was taken aback by his extensive knowledge of the area, including his understanding of the inner workings of the SPLA. He even knew the names of some SPLA generals who were lesser known beyond the borders of Sudan. Philippe wouldn't stop talking about Akobo, where he had been working on documentary projects.

I was soon on a plane to Los Angeles to audition solo, then it was back to New York to await further communication. Once Reese Witherspoon was available to audition, they flew me back out. Philippe pulled me aside and said that even if it wasn't an actual part, there would still be something for me in this movie about my country.

But I knew Philippe wanted me to put my all into the audition—I could hear it in his voice. I was introduced to Reese, who was kind and courteous and made me feel as though we were long-lost friends. The rest of the crew also treated me like I was already part of the team and auditions were just a formality. There was a sense I got that the crew felt like I could be even more useful to them than just as a cast member. They kept asking questions whenever I told them about my journey, from being a child soldier to walking the New York fashion runways.

In a few days, I got the call: they had selected me to play Jeremiah. I was at a loss for words. This was a big part—bigger than the ones I had auditioned for! Because I wasn't reacting to the news in any way, Philippe explained that Jeremiah was meant to be someone persuasive, someone who convinces people that there's a God. Philippe said he might not believe in God, but that when he saw me being persuasive, he thought he could be convinced. That's why he'd picked me.

Still unable to catch my breath, I just thanked Philippe and Mindy for the exhilarating news. Within a week, I flew to Atlanta and got down to work on the film. My friend Emmanuel Jal was also cast in the movie, as were two more South Sudanese actors, Arnold Oceng and Kuoth Wiel. We shot in Atlanta before proceeding to Cape Town, South Africa, where we filmed many of the Africa-based scenes. We also shot scenes in Nairobi and in the Kakuma refugee camp in northern Kenya, giving the cast and crew a feel for what life was like for refugees.

I took every opportunity to recount my experiences growing up. Because of this, the cast and crew took the film more seriously, and the director and producers brought me and Emmanuel on board as consultants to ensure the story was told accurately.

Throughout filming, I beamed and sometimes cried whenever I recalled wrestling with my brothers Duany, Chuol, and Oder and my cousin Wunbil in the black, incredibly fertile earth on the banks of the Nile, the same black color of our skin. I, the boy who never truly had a home, had now become a man at home all over the world. Wherever I went, I carried my blackness, the color of my homeland—a constant reminder that peace and rebirth were possible. I had built myself a remarkable life, starting with nothing but hope.

Being part of this incredible film and having the producers respect my expertise on South Sudan—its politics and its people—was one of the greatest experiences of my life. Once again, I felt deeply connected to my past and community. I had gone from being a small boy caught in a web of unspeakable violence to a respected voice on the struggles in my homeland. Once a child soldier wielding an AK-47, I now saw myself as an ambassador of peace, armed with a hopeful story of triumph, which I was eager to tell anyone willing to hear and learn from it.

With the establishment of the new government of the Republic of South Sudan under way, many of my contemporaries from the Sudanese diaspora were moving back home. Those outside government set up shop in the private sector, including business, academia, and the media. There had been a running joke that South Sudan was a country without a state. Now the work of state building had fallen upon us, and everyone was rolling up their sleeves.

But despite all this good energy, there arose murmurs about corruption and excess. The joke that started making the rounds was that other African countries had corruption, but South Sudan had pure looting. A new, flashy South Sudanese elite was forming, known for their selective largesse and over-the-top lifestyles. The general feeling among civilians and government officials was that it was taking longer for ordinary people to reap the rewards of independence. The perpetual promise was that once systems were established and functioning, the people in the villages, like Akobo, would get a taste of our newfound milk and honey. But oil money was leaking.

I was in Juba in March 2012, when what appeared to be the new republic's first political and economic crisis came knocking. Sudan and South Sudan engaged in territorial clashes over oil, which led South Sudan to shut down oil production, heavily curtailing its revenue and resulting in loss of life and property. Peace prevailed months later, and it was back to business as usual, though some serious damage had been done.

More cracks started emerging within the SPLA, pitting South Sudan's president, Salva Kiir Mayardit, against his vice president, Dr. Riek Machar. There had been serious teething problems in transforming the SPLA from a liberation movement into a properly functioning political party, and there was a growing sense that the president, being its de facto leader and commander in chief, was trying to lock out any competition for party leadership. Soon the power struggle within the SPLA took an ethnic turn, with the Dinka president retreating to his ethnic base to drum up military support in preparation for what seemed like an inevitable confrontation with the Nuer vice president. And there were also other figures jockeying for the SPLA's top leadership and the country's presidency, including the much-respected "Mama" Rebecca Nyandeng, Dr. John Garang's widow.

I was leaving Nairobi for New York on July 23, 2013, when I received news that President Kiir had dismissed Dr. Machar from office. I immediately sensed trouble brewing, knowing how ethnically dicey my country's politics were. In December 2013, President Kiir accused Dr. Machar and ten other leading SPLA figures of plotting a military coup to oust him. Dr. Machar denied involvement and fled Juba, only to reemerge, leading an armed splinter group within the SPLA called the SPLA in Opposition.

This set the stage for the start of a new civil war, largely viewed through the prism of a renewed Dinka-Nuer rivalry, one ethnic group dominating the government forces and the other dominating the opposition forces. Long-winded international mediation led to the signing of a peace accord in August 2015, which saw Dr. Machar's return to the vice presidency in a power-sharing agreement. But the peace didn't hold for long. Dr. Machar's home in Juba, among others, was flattened by government forces, resulting in hundreds of deaths in what seemed like targeted killings of the Nuer. A new phase of the war broke out, with Dr. Machar and other leading SPLA figures fleeing into exile. A tenuous peace agreement was later signed, and Dr. Machar was sworn in as first vice president of the unity government, officially ending the civil war. But sporadic fighting and occasional atrocities continue today.

To me, it was like the ouroboros, the snake that eats its own tail. We were back to square one: war and suffering.

Shortly after I finished shooting *The Good Lie,* I received a phone call from my old friend Jangjuol, whom Paul had sent back to Akobo. Trying to retrace his steps back to Ethiopia and find a way to America, Jangjuol had found a group with which he could travel to Walda, where he would survive a season's cattle rustling and the abduction of several children. He had then received sponsorship to immigrate to the United States, just like the rest of us had. He now lived in Salt Lake City, Utah, with his wife and five children.

I hopped on a plane and met his warm and bubbly family. Afterward, Jangjuol and I had a moment to ourselves. We sat outside an Ethiopian restaurant, just like we did back in the day, while eating injera with shiro and *thiem,* cubes of seasoned meat. I told him I had recently spoken to Garang Barjok, the only one of our boyhood friends I hadn't heard from in a long time. He had seen me on television doing an interview, and though he was now a colonel in the SPLA, he burst into tears seeing how much trouble I'd gone through in order to speak about what we all went through.

Jangjuol and I laughed about how difficult adjusting to American life could be, how far we had come, and how it was all worth it. Then, suddenly, Jangjuol stopped mid-laugh.

JANGJUOL: Believe me, brother. I paid for this with my soul.

I related to what he was saying. Being a refugee forces you to remake yourself a thousand times in a thousand different ways, despite your trying to hold on to some piece of yourself that you think makes you you. That night, as I sat there with Jangjuol, my heart was filled with warmth and gratitude. Despite everything, we had both managed to carve out our own place in a world that so often made out like it didn't want us. We'd survived, become our own men, and found our way back to each other—and ourselves—walking toward the rising sun.

ACKNOWLEDGMENTS

I would like to thank my father and mother, who brought me into this world and cultivated intrinsic value within me during Sudan's civil war. I am grateful for my siblings, some dead and some alive. I think of you in all that I do, knowing that you watch and pray over me.

I am indebted to many of my friends. You know who you are. I would like to thank filmmaker Wanuri Kahiu and her husband, Dr. Anthony Gikonyo, of the Karen Hospital, for your invaluable support to my family during my wife's risky pregnancy and the birth of my firstborn son, Hoaw Ger Duany.

I would like to express my appreciation to my co-writers, Garen Thomas and Isaac Amuke Otide. You are both blessed with the unique gift of storytelling and a keen intelligence to navigate through my many years and capture the essence of me. I am lucky to have had Garen Thomas and the great effort she made refining raw and unfiltered material.

To my literary agent, Todd Shuster, who encouraged me to tell my story. And that's what education should truly be about: human stories.

I am grateful to Chris Myers and Michelle Frey for advising me on the importance of process. It is a privilege to team up with the smartest people in the literary world. Thank you to editor Arely Guzmán; copyeditors Artie Bennett, Iris Broudy, Amy Schroeder, and Nancee Adams; managing editor Jake Eldred; publisher Melanie Nolan; designer Angela Carlino; and Yvan Alagbé for the spectacular artwork. Also, thanks to the publicity, marketing, and social media teams, including Mary McCue, Kristopher Kam, Jules Kelly, Kelly McGauley, Kate Keating, Adrienne Waintraub, and Kristin Schulz. Thanks to my publisher, Alfred A. Knopf and Make Me a World, under Penguin Random House, for always lending me an ear. This memoir would not be possible without your support.

I am amazed as I look at the incredible amount of change that has occurred in my four decades of life. I am grateful for what I've been granted thus far and I look forward to years ahead. I welcomed my firstborn son into the world in 2019. His journey will become a part of mine, and mine a part of his. In this book, I have opened up to share with you the many horrors and difficulties I faced on this long journey, from my time as a child soldier and refugee of war to the countless times I should have died but somehow survived. I've come to learn that all experiences are equally important. I've had some success, thrills, and triumphs on my journey. The good could not exist without the bad.

I have worn and exhausted many labels throughout my life so far: "War Child," "Refugee," "Lost Boy of Sudan," "Immigrant," "American High School Student," "College Athlete," "University Graduate," "Fashion Model," "Hollywood Actor," "Activist," "Speaker," "UNHCR Goodwill Ambassador," and now "Author." These labels represent how others have seen me during different parts of my journey. As you read about my life as a whole, with all its ups and downs, I think you will realize that I am simply a person, like you, who has collected an abundance of suffering, hard work, hope, positive thinking, faith, good luck, and success, and mixed all these ingredients into a life that I hope is continuing to positively impact humanity.

After that horrible day of separation by the Nile, it took nearly twenty years before I finally returned to Greater Akobo to reunite with my family. Three years later, I returned to the Kakuma, Ifo, and Itang refugee camps, where I had come from twenty-nine years earlier. But this time I was there as a Hollywood actor filming *The Good Lie*, a major studio project that closely mirrored my own life in countless ways, with famed actress Reese Witherspoon. The experience of being back in a refugee camp was therapeutic, but it was hard to process at times. Why? My horizons had broadened. My perspective had changed along this journey. I was a very different man, and yet I was still somehow in touch with little me from my past, the innocent boy who loved his family, his people, and the simple village life; the little boy who could find inspiration and possibility in the dark Sudanese mud waiting to be molded by a pair of creative hands.

I pray these stories about my journey will engage, entertain, and galvanize you. May all of our journeys continue toward the rising sun.